M000228502

FRANCIS OF ASSISI
Messenger for Today's World

FRANCIS OF ASSISI
Messenger for Today's World

by
Robert Waldron

New City Press
Hyde Park, New York

Published by New City Press
202 Comforter Blvd., Hyde Park, NY 12538
www.newcitypress.com
©2019

Cover design & book layout by Miguel Tejerina

Francis of Assisi: Messenger for Today's World.
by Robert Waldron

Library of Congress Control Number: 2019943946

978-1-56548-689-8 paperback
978-1-56548-690-4 e-book

Printed in the United States of America

Bellini's Francis

Hurt hard by prayer, Francis
staggers, sways. The very Love
that draws him, stays him now,
and shocks with sudden pain.
His hands are holes. His quick feet,
nailed to stone, hold him here.

Far off, a shepherd stares, his flock
astir, his flock afraid. A heron,
practiced in stillness, waits.
With pity, a hare looks up
at Francis from his little cell.

The donkey, used to burdens,
recalls Francis' Friend,
the Babe he warmed with breath,
the Man who rode his back
through waving palms,
through songs and shouts,
Who also came to this.

Francis gasps. He sees through tears
what we can't see. What seems a bright
dancing tree, what seem white cloths
of sunlit cloud, is One he's come to love
more truly now, in his pierced and grieving
heart, in all his life and limb.[1]

James Littwin

Contents

Introduction

When pursuing spiritual renewal, there is no better companion for the journey than Francis of Assisi, the *Poverello*—the "little poor man"—the world's most beloved and popular saint. Francis is famous for many reasons. He was a gentle man of the Middle Ages, a troublesome time when the gentle were crushed beneath the feet of the proud, the powerful, and the avaricious. He was a man in love with Christ, offering himself completely to the Man of Sorrows.

Growing up in a privileged and wealthy home, Francis (the name his father gave him, but his mother chose Giovanni, after St. John the Baptist) stripped himself of all worldly encumbrances to embrace Lady Poverty. Although he had a phobia of sick people, particularly lepers, he devoted his life to helping the poor, the ill, the hungry, the lowest of the low, the world's pariahs (including lepers, though he kept his distance until the day he kissed one).

He had only three years of formal education, but possessed the soul of a poet, softening the hardest of heart with his songs and verses, words that praised the beauty of God's creation. He once yearned for glory as a knight, but became a passionate knight for Christ, devoting himself not to warfare but to peace, without and within; he loved Christ so wholly and holily that Christ honored him by bestowing upon him the stigmata, open wounds like those that shed the divine blood that saves the world.

As we begin a new millennium, we want to reintroduce St. Francis to a new generation of Christians and non-Christians. Why? Because no other saint so completely embraced Jesus Christ. Francis's life was not an *imitatio Christi*; it was far more profound than imitation. Francis disappeared into Christ to such an extent that he could say, "Not I, but Christ in me" (Gal:2:20). As much as a person can become Christ, Francis did.

9

In the past, almost every Catholic knew who St. Francis was. He was the son of Pietro Bernadone of Assisi, born in 1182 and died in 1226. He founded the Order of Friars Minor (O.F.M.), popularly known as "Franciscans." In 1228, two years after his death, Pope Gregory IX canonized him. From then on his fame, his spiritual message, and his religious order have spread throughout the world.

Our modern culture has reduced Francis to a gentle man who preached to birds. But he was far from sentimental. Yes, he was gentle and charming, and indeed possessed a mystical rapport with animals, particularly birds. But more importantly, within the Catholic Church he initiated a spiritual rebirth long before Martin Luther. Francis indeed obeyed the command heard from Christ in the church of Damiano: "Rebuild my church." And only a man who was committed, tough, and courageous, who did not fear poverty, disease, and abuse, could accomplish what Christ had asked of him.

Some people may ask how a twelfth-century figure can inspire us today. Francis is not only a man for the Middle Ages; he is also, to borrow playwright Robert Bolt's description of St. Thomas More, "a man for all seasons." Francis was a person of realism, one who today, because of the life he embraced, would be called a revolutionary. His life is far from over. Some say it has barely begun, because at its heart is the dilemma of universal poverty. Thus, to anyone who says "Another book about St. Francis?" we reply, "Thank God, for we cannot pigeonhole St. Francis according to time because he is timeless."

In Francis, every generation finds the saint they need. We shall see, however, that Francis himself does not change. The more we know about him, the more we open ourselves to change within us: if we pay attention to Francis's life and his spiritual message, in our time we will see with different, rinsed eyes, and we will find in him the message uniquely meant for us.

The ailments of the twelfth and thirteenth centuries mirror those of today—war, poverty, hunger, homelessness, and disease. Things have not changed much. As in the Middle Ages, our world is still divided into the haves and the have-nots. Christ himself reminds us, "You always have the poor with you" (Jn 12:8). Francis did not ignore these troubles. He faced them, trying to allay if not solve them, a huge task for one person. But with God's help he was able to assist many of God's people. And because he could speak with those who had suffered during his time and connect with them, he can speak to us.

Our world still has millions of hungry, homeless, war-scarred, disease-ridden children, women, and men. Francis extends his stigmatized hands across the centuries to help us face life, to lift our spirits, to help us discover what is real in life; he also points his finger toward Christ, who said, "I am the light of the world. Whoever follows me will never walk in darkness but will have the light of life" (Jn 8:12).

In his way of life, Francis shows us the way to Christ. He speaks to us now in our moment. He himself is the example par excellence of a person who not only emulates but becomes Christ. Thus, to listen to and follow Francis is to listen to and follow Christ, ultimately to become Christ-like.

We will always need role models to help us live Christian lives; for this very reason Holy Mother Church has created a pantheon of saints, for she knows that we need to identify with real people. The true purpose of sainthood is not to glorify any human being, but to present exemplars of holiness to help to bring each of us to Christ. For nine hundred years, Francis has done this.

There is, indeed, a Franciscan spirituality. To learn about it and so apply it to our lives we need to know Francis's story. We need to know about his wild youth, about his conversion, about the vicissitudes of separating himself from his family, about the difficulties of establishing his religious order, about his struggles to become more Christ-like, and about his inner battles to preserve the purity of his mind and soul. We will learn about his gentle disposition, his love of nature, his love of animals, his love of prayer, and above all, his love of Jesus Christ who bathes our souls.

We will do this by looking at images. Each of the five chapters will begin with a stanza from St. Francis's "The Canticle of the Creatures." This poem, composed late in his life, expresses the core of Franciscan spirituality. To touch Francis, like the woman who touched the hem of Christ's tunic, we need only read and meditate upon his Canticle; it will place us first in his presence, and then in the presence of God. The Canticle will touch us with Francis's message, and will transform our lives as Christians.

Another aid to understanding Francis and his spiritual way is Bellini's famous *St. Francis in the Desert* (also called *St. Francis in Ecstasy*), which many consider the world's greatest painting. The original is in the Frick Museum, New York City.

We can learn much about Francis and his spirituality by meditating upon Bellini's masterpiece, and so we will make frequent reference to it. It reveals what Francis considered important in life and provides an entrance into the mystery of his life and being, one like no other saint venerated in the Catholic Church.

Francis will always remain an enigma, but by employing study, prayer, and meditation on his life and on his modern and unique message, we will find in him the saving word meant individually for each of us on our once-only life journey.

Francis was a builder. As a young man, he learned masonry while tearing down Assisi's La Rocca Castle and reusing the stones to build a city wall. Thus, when from the Byzantine cross in the ruined church of San Damiano in Assisi Christ asked Francis to rebuild his church, he meant not only the small, decrepit structure, but also the troubled, chaotic universal Church. Francis rebuilt San Damiano as well as two other churches, San Pietro della Spina and the "Porziuncola," the little structure enclosed within Santa Maria degli Angeli. It became the cradle of the Franciscan movement. An expert at rebuilding churches made of stone as well as the earthly Church, Francis can also help to rebuild Christian lives.

Everything great begins small. A painting begins with a brushstroke, a sculpture with the stroke of a hammer on a chisel, a musical composition with a note, a poem with a word, a novel with a sentence, a dance with a step. Discovering the charming, joyful, holy St. Francis begins with turning one page to the next. Each small gesture has the power to change one's life forever.

This book can be used on your own, or with a group. Either approach is beneficial. The book is designed to be read over the course of five weeks, one chapter a week. Each concludes with study guide questions meant to lead readers, individually or in a group, more deeply into Francis's life and message, bringing you closer to the saint and so closer to Christ.

The Canticle of the Creatures

Most high, all powerful, all good Lord!

All praise is Yours, all glory, all honor, and all blessing.

To You, alone, Most High, do they belong.

No mortal lips are worthy to pronounce Your name.

Be praised, my Lord, through all Your creatures, especially through my lord Brother Sun, who brings the day; and You give light through him.

And he is beautiful and radiant in all his splendor!

Of You, Most High, he bears the likeness.

Be praised, my Lord, through Sister Moon and the stars; in the heavens You have made them bright, precious and beautiful.

Be praised, my Lord, through Brothers Wind and Air, and clouds and storms, and all the weather, through which You give Your creatures sustenance.

Be praised, my Lord, through Sister Water; she is very useful, and humble, and precious, and pure.

Be praised, my Lord, through Brother Fire, through whom You brighten the night.

He is beautiful and cheerful, and powerful and strong.

Be praised, my Lord, through our sister Mother Earth, who feeds us and rules us, and produces various fruits with colored flowers and herbs.

Be praised, my Lord, through those who forgive for love of You; through those who endure sickness and trial.

Happy those who endure in peace, for by You, Most High, they will be crowned.

Be praised, my Lord, through our sister Bodily Death, from whose embrace no living person can escape.

Woe to those who die in mortal sin!

Happy those she finds doing Your most holy will.

The second death can do no harm to them.

Praise and bless my Lord, and give thanks, and serve Him with great humility.[2]

Chapter One

Francis's Youth and the Voice from the Cross of San Damiano

Most high, all powerful, all good Lord!
All praise is Yours, all glory, all honor, and all
   blessing.
To You, alone, Most High, do they belong.
No mortal lips are worthy to pronounce Your name.
Be praised, my Lord, through all Your creatures,
   especially through my lord Brother Sun, who
   brings the day; and You give light through him.
And he is beautiful and radiant in all his splendor!

"The Canticle of the Creatures"

1

The Canticle of the Creatures

We begin our journey with "The Canticle of the Creatures," a poem that reflects many remarkable facts. Francis
composed it at the end of his life. The zenith of his mystical
journey, his reception of the stigmata at Mount La Verna, had left him quite ill. He was nearly blind; his disease
made him sensitive to any illumination, from sunlight to
the mere flame of a candle.

Thomas of Celano, his biographer, records how this
poem of praise welled up within Francis after he had received the stigmata and returned to Assisi:

> One night when Francis was exhausted
> more than usual because of his severe in-
> firmities, he nevertheless kept the shield
> of patience unshaken by praying to Christ.
> Finally, as he prayed in agony, the Lord
> gave him this promise of eternal life. "If the
> whole bulk of the earth and the whole uni-
> verse were made of precious gold without
> price, and it was given to you as a reward for
> these severe sufferings which you are now
> enduring, and instead you would be given a
> treasure of such great glory, in comparison
> with which that gold would be as nothing,
> not even worthy of mention, would you not
> be happy and would you not willingly bear
> what you are bearing?"
>
> "I would indeed be happy," Francis replied,
> "and I would rejoice beyond all measure."
>
> "Rejoice!" the Lord exclaimed, "for your
> sickness is a promise of my kingdom. There-
> fore await your inheritance of the kingdom,
> steadfast and assured, because of the merit
> of your patience."[3]

Soon after this declaration, Francis composed "The
Canticle of the Creatures" at San Damiano, where St. Clare
and her nuns maintained a convent and a hospital. In his
final painful days they cared for him as he endured a number of serious ailments, including trachoma, an eye disease
he likely contracted when he visited Egypt. Paradoxically,
while almost blind Francis composed the Canticle, one of
the first poems in vernacular Italian, in praise of the visible

glory of God's creation. It conveys such pure joy that one wonders how a man so ill could be so happy and articulate.

Francis could praise God because he himself had disappeared into God, a continuation of the unitive experience of Mount La Verna; whatever Francis uttered was inspired. In fact, one could say that he served as the mouthpiece of God, who looks at creation through Francis and, as in Genesis, finds it "very good" (Gn 1:31). Keep in mind, however, that when Francis "looks" with his inner eye he is seeing the beauty of the world imprinted upon his mind and soul, for his physical eyes could no longer tolerate light.

"The Canticle of the Creatures," a mystically charged poem from the medieval era, speaks eloquently and meaningfully to contemporary readers, who are far more attuned to ecology. Unlike the audience in Francis's time, we recognize how we have damaged God's earth.

The poem begins with distance—the Lord God is "most high." Francis is looking up at the sun's golden disc, far above human beings and all other earthly creatures. By so quickly rendering the distance Francis emphasizes his own lowliness. He then lists all of life's worthiest attributes—praise, glory, honor, and blessing—as belonging alone to the Most High. Nothing is greater than God.

Humbled by God's greatness, Francis announces that no mortal is worthy to pronounce God's name. Spatial distance is added to spiritual distance: human beings are far removed from God yet they live in the light of the sun, in the presence of God. Hence, in praising God and all creatures, Francis begins with Brother Sun. From a medieval perspective he renders the sun, who brings the light that produces all we need to live, as masculine. But he also describes the sun as "fair," that is, beautiful. The sun shines with "splendor," that is, with magnificence. So Francis is saying that every virtue attributed from time immemorial to the sun belongs first to God. And echoing St. Augustine's dictum that God is the source of all beauty, praise in the Canticle implies that the beauty of the cosmos can mirror only in small measure qualities that God alone possesses. Nothing is higher or more beautiful than the Most High.

How does this stanza resonate with us today? In our world, the ego has won dominance. We cater to our every whim. We deny ourselves nothing. We see ourselves as the center of the world, the universe, the cosmos. But the Canticle reminds us of our true place in all of creation. As St. Nicholas of Cusa notes, "God is a circle whose center is everywhere, whose circumference is nowhere."[4]

Although he underscores our distance from the sun, Francis implies intimacy by referring to it as "brother," a word that calls to mind *philia*, brotherly love. Because Francis regards the sun as his brother, he does not fear its power and splendor. In fact, praising Brother Sun makes him feel comfortable and reassured. Keep in mind that he is composing this poem in his imagination: he is now almost blind. Thus, into his mind's eye he raises the radiance of the sun that had been stamped into his mind and soul. God alone can imprint such images upon us. And the sun reminds Francis of his Lord Christ, "the Light of the World" (Jn 8:12).

How can this poem's genesis not inspire us? A person wracked with pain, who can do nothing for himself, who must be fed, cleaned, clothed by others, with his inner eye still "sees" immense beauty in the world. Francis's body was crumbling like the ruined Church of San Damiano, but the spirit of God in Christ never departed from him: "I will be with you always" (Mt: 28:20).

2

Biography

Famous historical figures can be hidden under layers of mythology, legend, and apocryphal stories. It is challenging to discern the true person, especially for someone who lived nine hundred years ago. We must seek to discover what Thomas Merton calls the True Self of Francis, but doing so requires stripping away of some of the masks history has imposed upon him and establishing an informed, well-researched background. Sometimes we will need to speculate, but when we do, it will be well-informed and will avoid the air of dogmatic certainty.

Francis left very little that he composed himself. There are two brief hand-written items, but everything else that bears his name was dictated. These documents include his *First Rule* for the Franciscan Order, which was superseded by a shorter *Second Rule*. A *Third Rule* was composed by other Franciscans, its original length cut in half although Francis's spirit was retained. This *Rule* was approved by Pope Honorius III in 1223. In his forties Francis dictated his *Testament* while physically ill. He dictated "The Canticle of the Creatures" (also known as "The Canticle to the Sun") in a spurt of inspiration. Thomas of Celano composed several biographies (called legends), which were superseded by Bonaventure's, requested and approved by Pope Gregory IX and gladly accepted by the Franciscan Order. Although Bonaventure never met Francis, his is still considered the definitive biography. He greatly revered Francis, believing that when he was a young boy his ill health was cured through prayers to Francis of Assisi.

We can say with certainty that after Francis's death those in authority, both in Rome and in the Franciscan Order, made every effort to control and promulgate a certain image of Francis: a saintly one. During his lifetime Francis himself considered his youth to have been sinful, repeating that characterization in his *Testament*. Yet his followers and champions (some of them popes) have maintained that saintly image, avoiding exploration of his "sinful" youth.

Hollywood could not have done a better job in promoting the saintly image of Francis than did these followers and champions. His youth did not seem as wild and profligate as Augustine's or Thomas Merton's, both of whom fathered children early in their lives. It is likely that Francis's youth was similar, although he never got a girl pregnant. In his forties, however, hearing his brothers speaking about his holiness, Francis reminded them that he was still capable of fathering a child. What did he actually mean by such a statement? He meant that his sexuality was still alive, that he was still a vibrant, virile man, still attracted to women. Although certainly a saint, Francis was a person like us—not the familiar sentimental picture of a charming, somewhat sexless young man preaching to the birds or talking to a wolf.

We need to understand Francis as one of us, for in fact he was one of us. As a teenager he would have fit well into any modern adolescent clique. Like today's young people, he liked expensive clothes (and his father, a cloth merchant, made sure he had them); he liked music, partying, drinking; he would stay up until all hours of the night with his pals, and he likely fell into a drunken sleep in many an Assisi doorway, awakening with a hangover, then staggering home through the early dawn and falling into bed to sober up. From time immemorial young men have traversed such a rite of passage.

Thomas of Celano writes,

> This is the wretched early training in which that man whom we today venerate as a saint—for he truly is a saint—passed his time from childhood and miserably wasted and squandered his time almost up to the

twenty-fifth year of his life. Maliciously advancing beyond all of his peers in vanities, he proved himself a more excessive inciter of evil and a zealous imitator of foolishness. He was an object of admiration to all, and he endeavored to surpass others in his flamboyant display of vain accomplishments: wit, curiosity, practical jokes and foolish talk, songs and soft and flowing garments. Since he was very rich, he was not greedy but extravagant, not a hoarder of money but a squanderer of his property, a prudent dealer but a most unreliable steward.[5]

Celano's description of Francis does not shock audiences now as it would have in the past. Contemporary psychology, especially adolescent psychology, considers such behavior with more compassion. In fact, Thomas of Celano's words fit many a teenager today. Francis's adolescence can be interpreted from a psychoanalytic perspective. In their wild behavior he and his friends are exhibiting a crisis of identity. Erik H. Erikson writes:

The identity crisis occurs in that period of the life cycle when each youth must forge for himself some central perspective and direction, some working unity, out of the effective remnants of his childhood and the hopes of his anticipated adulthood; he must detect some meaningful resemblance between what he has come to see in himself and what his sharpened awareness tells him others judge and expect him to be.[6]

Pietro Bernadino, a successful cloth merchant, showered upon Francis and his other son, Angelo, whatever they wanted or needed or even did not need. He had hoped Francis would follow in his footsteps to run his thriving business, eventually taking it over when Pietro was too old to do so.

Francis is often described as "a man without learning" because he had only three years of formal education. But he was highly intelligent, poetically gifted and quick-witted, and a good student of business. He worked in his father's enterprise, traveling with him by horse to fairs at Spoleto, Foligno, and other places throughout Italy. He learned not only how to make money but also how to spend it, lavishly entertaining his young friends with wine and food. He was fluent in French, learned from having traveled there often with his father and from his mother singing him many a song in her native tongue.

Francis was said to have "leaky hands" because of his generosity to his friends and also to the poor; he had always possessed great compassion for beggars. Once while busy at work in his father's store, Francis sent away a mendicant who showed up at the door. But he quickly regretted his unkindness. Realizing that he would never have responded in such a brusque and uncharitable fashion to one of his no-ble friends seeking a loan, he ran after the beggar to make amends. He maintained such love for the poor throughout his life, to the point that he would eventually choose to become one of them. Raised in luxury with every desire indulged, he chose to devote his life to living among the poorest, serving and loving them.

This son of a cloth merchant was the best-dressed young man in Assisi. According to Thomas of Celano, he was slender, with a kindly and comely countenance accent-ed by a scanty beard, and a strong, musical voice. No doubt he turned the heads of many a young woman in Assisi and beyond. Being charming, well-dressed, and fun-loving, he naturally drew many friends.

Although Francis was middle class, his friends often were from the noble class, which pleased his father. As fathers often do, he wanted his son to develop connec-tions and perhaps marry well. Had he wanted to, Francis could have had a privileged life among his noble friends; instead, he chose his companions from among the lowest of the low, emulating Christ, the one upon whom he based his life.

His friends were well-known for awakening the people of Assisi with their laughter, singing, and noisy drunken taunting. With gusto, they sang popular songs beneath the windows of attractive young women. In his pleasant voice, Francis—Vachel Lindsay called him "God's Troubadour"—led his friends in the Franco-Italian lyrics popularized by the jongleurs, the interpreters of the troubadours.

Francis dreamed of winning glory as a knight, for he had no intention of following in his father's footsteps. Like many young men he dreamed of adventure in war. What generation has not viewed combat as a way to prove manhood and to win glory? Even today young people volunteer for the military out of duty and necessity, or for adventure, or to test their skills and courage. Francis, a young man of the twelfth century, was no different.

The opportunity for military service soon presented itself. On the horizon loomed a war with Assisi's ancient enemy, Perugia. In 1201, when Francis was twenty years old, Assisi attacked Perugia, primarily to win back the property of Perugians living in Assisi that had been lost in a previous war against German princes. Francis was taken prisoner in 1202 at the battle of Ponte San Giovanni. After more than a year, he was finally ransomed by his still-adoring father.

In prison Francis charmed other inmates, most of them sons of nobility, keeping them from succumbing to depression and despair. He used his winning personality to convince them to accept and to embrace an unlikable young knight whom everyone else shunned because of his vain, complaining, and unpleasant personality.

His imprisonment, however, ruined Francis's health. Back in Assisi, he needed a year of bed-rest to recuperate. In prison, without decent food and clean water, it is likely that he contracted typhoid or malaria as well as tuberculosis. It marked the beginning of Francis's lifelong poor health, for he rarely took heed of "Brother Ass" (his body), devoting it unceasingly to God's work, even subjecting it to severe spiritual asceticism.

At night the young Francis, gentle, charming, dressed in silks and finery, rings on his fingers, wandered the streets in a wine haze. As an adult, after embracing Christ at twenty-five years old, he subjected his body to an asceticism that today would be considered unhealthy if not reckless. Keep in mind, however, that in the Middle Ages people thought that the pursuit of holiness demanded punishment of the body, which was considered the enemy of the spirit. This belief stems from the Platonic philosophy that influenced the early Church, which understood the human person to be composed of body and soul. The soul, being immortal, was the source of goodness and purity, but because of its unruly desires the body was held in a distrust bordering on contempt (see Plato's *Phaedrus*).

The Platonic view of the human body has been supplanted today by a healthier and liberating Incarnational theology, which sees the body as holy not only because it is the temple of the Holy Spirit but also because Jesus Christ himself chose to inhabit a human body. He who was both human and divine experienced all that human beings experience. How can the body be evil, therefore, if God chose to be incarnated in one? But Francis, a medieval personality, always referred to his body as Brother Ass.

After a year-long convalescence, his psychological identity crisis still unresolved, Francis lost his purpose in life. He had hoped to win glory as a knight, but that dream was dashed into the bloody ground of battle and into the dark dungeon where he had spent an entire year. What happened to Francis during his year of recuperation? His biographers make no mention of him beginning to search for Christ or to pursue holiness. Probably, he was depressed. When he finally could step outside his home, he wandered into the nearby countryside, whose beauty had always lifted his spirits; but now it did nothing for him. The fields of poppies and other flowers, the abundant vineyards, the bright sun failed to delight him. How could they when his one great dream had been crushed? Now frail, he regarded himself at age twenty-two as a failure. But after his negativity abated, he again joined his friends and their nocturnal revels as he had done as a teenager.

In 1205, Francis decided to travel with a nobleman to join the forces of Walter of Brienne, placing himself under the leadership Pope Innocent III, who had called for a fourth Crusade and for another campaign against Germany. Phoenix-like, Francis's dream of glory arose from its own ashes. He dreamed of being in a room filled with armor, saddles, shields, and spears, all imprinted with the sign of the cross.

He set out from Assisi dressed in the most expensive fashion and with God's approval, granted to him in a dream. He embarked with the fervor of a soldier of Christ, eager to conquer the pope's enemies and to recapture the Holy Land from the Muslims. On his way, Francis met a poor knight wearing only the remnants of what had once been a glorious uniform. He had lost everything. Francis stripped off his fine clothes and handed them to the knight. This was the first of several divestments that marked Francis's life, each marking an important psychological and spiritual development.

Francis got as far as Spoleto when the malarial fever he contracted in prison incapacitated him once again. It must have been humiliating to return to Assisi, to have everyone gazing upon this once-gorgeous flower of Assisi's youth who had dreamed of chivalric honor returning defeated, ruined. It seemed that whatever Francis attempted ended in failure.

Just before his return Francis heard a voice whose meaning at the time he could not fathom. Only in hindsight did he discern its message. The voice said, "Francis, where are you going like this?"

"I am going to fight in Apulia."

"Tell me," the voice said, "From whom can you expect most, the master or the servant?"

"From the master, of course!"

"Then why follow the servant, instead of the master on whom he depends?"

"Lord, what would You have me do?"

"Return to your own country. There it shall be revealed to you what you are to do, and you will come to understand the meaning of this vision."[7]

Francis was not dreaming or having a vision: he had actually heard a voice. And he would soon hear another.

Now, when Francis was twenty-three, and he remained frail and despondent. He did not wish to follow his father and become a cloth merchant. In fact, he had no goals. Many of his former friends had entered family businesses or had married and were starting families. Francis, still boyish, was trying to find his way.

Without goals or purpose, Francis reverted to his old ways. Like other unsettled and confused young men, he wandered the streets drinking and singing beneath the windows of pretty girls. One night, disgusted with his carousing, Francis drew away from his friends. One of them asked what he was thinking about—dreaming of marriage, perhaps? Francis replied, "I will take a bride—one more noble and more beautiful than you have ever seen!"[8] His comment must have been greeted with sarcastic whoops and laughter, his friends thinking, "There he goes again, dreaming of glory, this time not as soldier but as a lover."

Francis's comment could have been a boast to silence his friends, who saw his life as a debacle—an "I'll show them" comment. But it may be interpreted more positively, as arising from his deepest self, his True Self. Such words could indicate a desire to uplift himself, to find purpose in life, to find psychological wholeness and spiritual holiness. Those words probably spilled from him without thought; he himself may not have understood their significance. But often spontaneous comments contain the most insight and truth.

From a Jungian perspective, Francis was getting in touch with his inner anima, the feminine archetype every male possesses, just as every female possesses an inner male, her animus. And his anima is revealing herself in an oblique fashion: she will not be his wife, but she is beautiful, and will bestow upon him great wealth, not of the world but of the soul: she is Lady Poverty. At that time, however, Francis had only a vague idea of Lady Poverty's presence. He would come to know and love her intimately, but at that moment he remained confused, apathetic, sad, often depressed, a young man who had failed twice at fulfilling his dream of becoming a knight.

Not long after speaking these enigmatic words, Francis was walking a mile outside Assisi near a small, abandoned church. To escape the heat of the sun, Francis entered the ruins of San Damiano, its roof caving in, its beams rotting, its bricks turning to dust, its floors a myriad of rain puddles. One element of beauty, however, remained: above the crumbling altar hung a Byzantine cross of Christ crucified. Sitting in the church's cool darkness, he gazed upon Christ's kind and gentle face. The open eyes seemed to be looking directly at Francis. He suddenly heard these words from the cross: "Francis, don't you see that my house is being destroyed? Go, then, and rebuild it for me."[9]

This voice from the cross is paramount in the life of Francis of Assisi. For nearly a quarter century he had done nothing except to pursue pleasure and unrealistic, foolish dreams. And now Christ was asking him to rebuild his house. He took Christ's words literally: he was to rebuild San Damiano. The full import of what Christ was asking had not yet dawned on Francis. But from a psychological perspective, by asking Francis to rebuild his ruined church Jesus is speaking to a ruined young man. He is asking Francis to rebuild himself—his life and all that it entails. Christ wants Francis to fulfill his potential, to become his True Self.

Francis's heart leapt. In an instant he discovered his *raison d'etre*, a reason for which to live. He hurried from the church, knowing what he must do. He had never been lazy; he worked hard for his father, learning how to be a good businessman even though his heart was not in it. He also knew how to use his body and hands in hard labor. He had engaged in physical combat, and as a teenager he joined other men in tearing down the castle of La Rocca and re-using the rocks, stones, and boulders to build a wall around Assisi. Indeed, Francis knew how to build. He was on easy terms with a trowel, bricks, mortar, and tiles. Yes, he would rebuild San Damiano, make it beautiful again, render it worthy for the presence of Christ, the Lord.

The aimless young man found a purpose in life that energized him.

3

Bellini's *St. Francis In The Desert*

St. Francis in the Desert, also known as *St. Francis in Ecstasy*, is now in the Frick Collection, in New York City. From the time of its creation in the late fifteenth century until the end of the eighteenth century the painting was owned by a series of patrician Renaissance families. Henry Clay Frick purchased it from an English financier in 1915 and displayed it in his home with other Renaissance paintings.

For our discussion here, refer to the illustration on the cover.

The painting depicts Francis as an older man, perhaps in his early forties. He stands in an unearthly, radiant light with his arms stretched out welcomingly to receive, it seems, the sunlight; but it is not only sunlight that he is receiving. God is imprinting upon him the stigmata. Francis's biographer describes the event which, except for the six-winged seraph, is captured by Bellini: "He saw a Seraph having six wings, fiery as well as brilliant, descend from the grandeur of heaven. And when in swift flight, it had arrived at a spot in the air near the man of God, there appeared between the wings the likeness of a man crucified, with his hands and feet extended in the form of a cross and fastened to a cross."[10]

The painting reveals the wounds on Francis's hands and feet. When he was a young man roaming the Umbrian hills, Thomas Merton imagined what Francis is gazing upon:

> All day I stared out at the bare hills, at the wild, ascetic landscape. Somewhere out there, on one of those mountains, St. Francis had been praying and the seraph with the fiery, blood-red wings had appeared

before him with the Christ in the midst of
those wings. . . . [11]

The painting is set on a piece of land on Mount La Verna, granted to Francis by an admiring nobleman, a place
where he could retreat to be alone and pray. So famous had
he become for his preaching and his holiness, Francis could
not go anywhere without attracting a crowd. Note the huge
rocks behind him, washed by sunlight. The rocky hillside
recalls the masonry Francis handled in rebuilding San Damiano and two other churches. The protruding rocks also
suggest that this man had rebuilt his life; the Francis in the
painting is the antithesis of his young self.

He is pictured at the apex of his spiritual journey, receiving the stigmata. He is unified with God, totally given
to God, owning nothing, no longer clad in the silks, feath-
ers, and jewels of his youth but in a coarse brown tunic. His
feet are bare, his sandals tossed behind him. For a belt he
wears a rope-cord. His only companions are a rabbit peeping out of a hole, a heron and other birds, and a donkey
that he had ridden to Mount La Verna because he was too
weak and ill to travel by foot. The trees, one a laurel, recall
the tree on which Christ was hung.

This Francis is neither the playboy nor the ruined
young man of the ruined San Damiano. As Francis rebuilt
San Damiano with his hands, bloodying them with the
harsh work, with his own bloodied hands Christ has rebuilt
Francis. Bellini depicts this "rebuilt" Francis.

Notice how the painting is suffused with golden sunlight, recalling the opening stanzas of "The Canticle of
the Creatures." It was composed after Francis received
the stigmata, and Bellini likely knew the Canticle well. To
portray a saint in ecstasy, he had to convey the significance
of the sun in Francis's life, for with and through sunlight
God manifested himself to Francis, and manifests himself
to us. We cannot live without the sun, and we cannot live
without God.

In their essay, "St. Francis in the Desert: Technique and Meaning," art critics Susannah Rutherglen and Charlotte Hale explain the significance of light in this painting:

> The rarefied blue of Bellini's sky constitutes a pure medium for the movement of light, an otherworldly effulgence that issues in several directions from the painting's upper left-hand corner. The artist has summoned an extraordinary radiance that streams in rays, pools in resplendent clouds and disturbs the branches of the laurel. Coursing through the depths of the sky and diffusing into every corner of the landscape, this golden light evokes the fiery illumination that reputedly bathed Mount La Verna during the stigmatization and was depicted in paintings of the miracle from the thirteenth century onward.[12]

4

Study Guide

Form a study group to discuss the life of St. Francis of
Assisi. Select one member to facilitate discussion. Readers are free to reflect on the following questions with the
group or alone.

It is suggested to begin each session with the *Prayer of
St. Francis.* Although probably not written by Francis himself, it reflects his spirit. Mother Teresa of Calcutta, the
most moving exemplar of Franciscan spirituality of our
time, often prayed it, both publicly and privately.

Prayer of St. Francis

Lord, make me an instrument of your peace.
Where there is hatred, let me sow love.
Where there is injury, pardon.
Where there is doubt, faith.
Where there is despair, hope.
Where there is darkness, light.
Where there is sadness, joy.
O Divine Master, grant that I may not so much seek
to be consoled, as to console;
to be understood, as to understand;
to be loved, as to love.
For it is in giving that we receive.
It is in pardoning that we are pardoned,
and it is in dying that we are born to Eternal Life.

1. What does the first invocation of "The Canticle of the Creatures" reveal about Francis of Assisi the person?

2. What does it reveal about Francis of Assisi the saint?

3. How are Francis the person and Francis the saint one and the same?

4. What is the significance of the sun in the poem?

5. How does sunlight characterize each season of the year?

6. List as many different kinds of light as you can.

7. What is the significance of light in the poem?

8. How might Francis be said to have had an "identity crisis"?

9. How would Francis's behavior in streets of Assisi affect his parents?

10. How might Francis's father be responsible for his son's behavior?

11. Although he seemed to have been a dutiful Catholic who received the Eucharist at Easter, confessed serious sin, and was charitable to beggars, Francis was unhappy. At this time God does not seem to be a part of his life. How is Francis responsible for his unhappiness?

12. Why did Francis desire to be a knight? What does this desire reveal?

13. Identify the voices Francis hears. What is the source of these voices?

14. How does God intervene in Francis's life? To what extent does God speak in the "still, small voice" within him?

15. What is your first reaction to *St. Francis in the Desert*?

16. What in it do you find confusing?

17. Where do your eyes go first? Why do you think that is so?

18.   As your eyes explore the painting, what moves you?

19.   What inspiration(s) does the painting give you?

20.   How does this painting make you want to know more about St. Francis?

21.   How might the stigmata be miraculous? How might it be psychosomatic? If the latter, does it diminish the value or importance of the stigmata?

22.   What other figures in modern times have received the stigmata?

Chapter Two

St. Francis Stripping Himself Naked in the Piazza di Santa Maria Maggiore

Be praised, my Lord, through Sister Moon and the stars;
in the heavens You have made them bright, precious and beautiful.

"The Canticle of the Creatures"

1

The Canticle of the Creatures

Francis begins his praise of the Lord's creatures with those that provide light. First, the sun, then the moon and the stars. He demonstrates intimacy with the moon and stars by referring to them as "Sister." Although he does suggest that Sister Moon is his alone, his language reflects his lack of egoism and ownership. Francis owns nothing; he is poor, depending upon others for food. He participates in and shares the beauty of the world and the heavens with all of God's creatures. The moon and the stars shed their light for everyone's enjoyment, for they are beautiful as well as pragmatic; like the sun, they provide light to the world.

Why does he call the moon "Sister"? From time immemorial humankind has considered the moon as feminine.

The moon's light is softer and gentler than the sun's. It does not burn the skin like the sun's can.

The moon has its seasons; it changes by declining, and just before it seems to disappear, it resurrects. It is an image with which all people can identify. We all have our ebbs and flows, our settings and risings. Everyone experiences cycles of emotion, lows and highs, particularly women whose bodies follow a monthly cycle. Perhaps the moon reminded Francis of Christ, who comes to us as circular communion bread, and who like the moon disappeared in death and rose again.

This interpretation is suggested by Francis's poetic invocation. What he states is simple—the moon and stars are set "in the heavens." Who set them there? God. Thus, these images are daily reminders of the world's divine source of light and beauty. And they are located in the heavens, in God's kingdom.

Francis surely was aware of Christ's comment, "the kingdom of God is within you." Thus these images of the moon and the stars, archetypes imprinted upon the mind and soul, surfaced as he composed "The Canticle of Creatures" because consciousness is the *light* of awareness. Consequently, when Francis composed his Canticle, he was *enlightened*; he viewed the world with the clarity of God's instruments: sun, moon, and stars. Moreover, when Francis composed this poem, he was quite ill and nearly blind; he had to draw upon his inner memory of God's firmament.

Although the sun and the moon and the stars stand *above* Francis, they also reside *within* his soul; distance is nullified by intimacy. As a brother to the sun, moon, and stars Francis has an intimacy that is deeper than what other nature poets feel. Familiar "nature poets"—artists such as William Wordsworth, John Keats, Percy Bysshe Shelley, Robert Frost, Edward Thomas, Mary Oliver, Jane Kenyon, or Seamus Heaney—convey their appreciation of the natural world through close observation of it.

Francis, however, operates on a different and deeper level. He observes and appreciates nature, yes, but he also becomes part of nature: to the point he is *one* with it. More than a nature poet, he is a mystic poet. "The Canticle of the Creatures" leaves readers with a clearer idea not only of Francis's nature but also of God's. Through the creatures he observes, Francis disappears into God. Like those creatures, Francis becomes a vehicle through which God reveals his light. And how does Francis help us participate in the divine light? Through poetry: "In the beginning was the Word, and the Word was with God, and the Word was God" (Jn 1:1).

2

Biography

In the ruins of San Damiano Francis found his *raison d'etre*: to rebuild God's church. In the beginning, he took Christ's request literally: to repair that fallen-down building. What happened in the holy ambiance of San Damiano moved this young man at his core, psychologically and spiritually. Nothing short of an "earthquake" rocked Francis's soul, shaking the very foundations of his life. As he restored San Damiano he also rebuilt his life, one formerly founded on sand.

What indeed happened to Francis? He had entered the church to escape the sun and possibly to pray (though as a young man he was not known for his piety). His attraction to a small church in ruins reveals his inner self. For the rest of his life, ruins of another sort would always catch his eye and heart: people ruined by poverty, by illness, by pestilence, by war, by a hostile society.

He did not look like a person in ruins. He was a well-dressed, comely gentleman who seemed to have everything to make him happy. But the person who slipped into San Damiano was not happy. Perhaps he identified with the ruined church, abandoned by everyone, where no one worshiped; he felt that he belonged in a church in "disgrace" with the locals because he had become such a failure, a disappointment to his father, his mother, and his scores of friends. Once the toast of Assisi, Francis was now viewed as a joke, a clown; novelist Julian Green describes him as "God's Fool."

Imagine Francis falling to his knees and lifting his eyes to the only remnant of the church's former beauty, its Byzantine cross of Christ Crucified. And he prayed, for mercy and forgiveness. He prayed to turn his life of failure into something positive and useful. And Christ answered his prayer.

Of all people, why did Christ ask a failure like Francis to rebuild San Damiano? Surely Francis, who considered himself the biggest loser in Assisi, asked the same question of himself. Christ asked Francis *because* he indeed was a loser, a sinner, a prodigal son who had lived a debauched life. He had wasted his father's money pursuing pleasure, adorned himself in his father's expensive fabric to attract and impress everyone around him. Francis's ego craved having everyone's eyes focused on him alone, their ears on his beautiful singing voice, their attention on his gallantry as he went off to war against the Perugians and with the papal armies against the German emperor. But he had returned defeated, stripped of his fine clothes and armor. But like the father in the parable of the prodigal son, God forgives all. Francis, once "dead," is brought back to life by Christ asking him to rebuild his church.

God endows human beings with free will. Therefore, Francis could accept the call to rebuild San Damiano, or refuse. It is likely that he had grown up reciting the Lord's Prayer, uttering "Thy kingdom come, thy will be done on earth as it is in heaven." Francis may have remembered Christ in the Garden of Gethsemane praying that his chalice of suffering be taken away, but in the end he said, "Not what I want but what you want" (Mt 26:39).

Francis marries his will to Christ's. He assumes the responsibility of rebuilding San Damiano. Thus commences what Carl Jung calls *individuation*: the process of finding and becoming one's self. Having passed through an identity crisis, Francis now knows what he is to do with his life. Having turned his life over to Christ, he will be led by Christ himself through his ongoing individuation. Paradoxically, by embracing Christ Francis embraces his own true self. Only later will the import of this decision manifest itself.

Rebuilding a church demands something Francis does not have—money. So he "borrows" cloth from his father and rides to Foligno where he sells both his father's material and his horse. He even sells his own clothes and dons peasant garb. Returning to San Damiano he hands his purse to the church's old curate. The curate hesitates to take the money because he fears Francis's father, known for his foul temper; so Francis tosses the moneybag onto a windowsill and gets to work.

But this decision is mistaken. Francis had no right to sell his father's property, nor had he the right to sell the horse and clothes that his father had given him. Francis had to rebuild San Damiano from nothing, and that nothing is himself. He had to build by the sweat of his brow, by his muscles, by the strength and skill of his own hands, now gone soft. A sacred place cannot be restored with stolen goods or with ego. He would need time to comprehend this.

Pietro was infuriated by his son's actions in Foligno and his intention to rebuild San Damiano. He accosted Francis there, retrieved his money, and demanded that his son return home. Francis refused. He hid in a cave and began a life of prayer and penance. To discover his true identity he needed to take a journey into the cavernous darkness of his inner self: into his inner unconscious mind, the abode of archetypes.

The inner cave (the inner self) is the place for prayer, for being one with God. Francis found his new "home" in one of Umbria's many caves, with mice and rats his only company. Entering the cave symbolizes Francis's inner journey to the deepest parts of his own mind and soul, to face his own demons, the fears and anxieties that make up his archetypal shadow.

Jung describes the shadow as that self we do not want to be. Francis had to face his past, his sins, his omissions, his lost opportunities, his accrued waste of life. And he had to do this in a healthy fashion, for true mental and spiritual health lies in self-acceptance and in self-forgiveness. Francis had to be as kind to himself as he would be to the poor, to the lepers, to God's other creatures. Thus, in the deep, dark, pit-like cave, alone with himself, Francis had to come to terms with who he was and what God wanted of him. What he finally determined is quite simple: he wanted to follow in the steps of Jesus Christ. It sounds simple to follow Christ, but to do so means walking down the Via Dolorosa, the way of sorrow.

Christ is the Man of Sorrows.

Francis's earthly father, Pietro, still sought to control his twenty-five-year-old son. All his life Francis had abided in his father's home. Pietro had fed and dressed him; what money Francis had, he had received from his father. But having learned that Francis had sold his fabric as well as his horse, had given away his clothes, and was rebuilding San Damiano, Pietro had enough of his son's foolishness. When Francis emerged from his hiding place, his father sought to control his son's life by imprisoning him within his own home.

Pietro did have reasons for trying to command and control his son's life. Like the father of the prodigal son, he indeed loved his son and had granted his every desire. He was proud that Francis was the toast of Assisi, proud that he had noble friends, proud of Francis's business acumen, proud that he sought to be a knight. He overlooked Francis's spendthrift ways, his drunkenness, his tendency to throw away money by entertaining his friends and by giving it to the ubiquitous poor in the streets of Assisi and the countryside. He hoped that Francis would eventually settle down, work hard, choose a wife, and start his own family. How often a father might say of a troubled son, "He's just going through a phase." But not Francis.

Pietro observed a son out of control. Today, a father in Pietro's circumstances would seek to get his son into therapy as soon as possible. Pietro may have thought that his son was going mad; plenty of evidence pointed toward madness. On several occasions, children had stoned him, calling him a madman, especially when he returned from his second military endeavor dressed in rags, having given away his fine clothes to the defeated knight for whom Francis had shown great compassion.

The thirteenth century had no knowledge of psychological categories like "identity crisis" or "nervous breakdown." Had Francis experienced these? Perhaps. His mind and soul indeed were in conflict. Modern spiritual and psychological language might suggest that his superego (his conscience) had been chastising him for his dissolute life, in an inner conversation referred to in the *Testament* he composed in his forties. Francis never forgot his "sinful" youth and he never ceased reminding his brothers of it. He had a realistic understanding of himself, and—unlike others around him—he never considered himself a saint.

Pietro, a worldly person, had one principal concern— profit. He did not seem to acknowledge the spiritual dimension: God, grace, and prayer. He probably attended Mass on Sunday, ostentatiously dropping money into the poor box, but was not known to be particularly pious. In his son, he saw not a budding saint but a young man losing his mind, or perhaps absurdly playacting as a holy man by giving away all that Pietro had worked so hard to gain. He was not about to watch his son toss away hard-earned wealth.

At home, Pietro confined Francis in a room. We can imagine him screaming, thrashing his son to bring him to his senses. Unmoved, Francis devoted himself to prayer and fasting. When Pietro left on a business trip, Francis's mother, Pica, released him. When Pietro returned, he sought to use the law to rein Francis in and to retrieve money he stole, but the magistrates had no authority in familial disputes. Because Francis had given the money to a church, Pietro would have to turn to the Church for justice. That meant approaching Bishop Guido, considered a fair and honest man; he was the wealthiest man in Assisi and so knew the value of money. Pietro thought that Guido would take his side.

This led to one of the most riveting scenes in young Francis's life. People filled the piazza to watch the "show"— Pietro pleading to Bishop Guido for a judgment against his wayward son. He proclaimed how he had given Francis everything, had been a generous and loving father. Listening quietly, Francis would have been moved by his father's plea, seeing through the haze of anger his father's love for him. But Francis also had come to realize who his true Father is—: God.

The bishop was inclined to favor Pietro, knowing what a good father he had been and knowing full well Francis's youthful reputation and promising future. But when asked to defend himself, Francis did not fall into an eloquent argumentation. He chose to let his actions speak for themselves. In front of everyone, he stripped off his clothes and returned them as well as the money he had received from selling his father's property. Before everyone he stood naked until the bishop himself covered Francis with his mantle.

By removing his clothes, which represented his former self, Francis—like a newborn, naked baby—commenced a new life. Francis rejected all that his father stood for; elegant, expensive clothes no longer meant anything to him. He did not disparage them, but they clearly were no longer for him. As a beloved son of the Father, he had chosen a new life, antithetical to his earthly father's. He would clothe himself like the poor—barefoot, in a threadbare and patched brown tunic with a chalked cross on its back. He would live among the poor and the ill, feeding and caring for them. Francis, a new man, had a purpose and an example of life to follow: Jesus Christ's.

Everyone in the piazza, including the bishop, was moved by Francis's actions, more eloquent than anything that could be said. Actions reveal far more than words.

Thomas of Celano recounts the episode:

> When he was in front of the bishop, he neither delayed nor hesitated, but immediately

took off and threw down all his clothes and
returned them to his father. He did not even
keep his trousers on, and he was completely
stripped bare before everyone. The bishop,
observing his frame of mind and admiring
his fervor and determination, got up and,
gathering him in his own arms, covered him
with the mantle he was wearing. He clearly
understood that this was prompted by God
and he knew that the action of the man of
God, which he had personally observed,
contained mystery. After this he became his
helper. Cherishing and comforting him, he
embraced him in the depths of charity.[13]

Standing naked in the piazza, Francis must have felt a
lightness of being. By shedding his clothes he had dropped
all the burdens he had been carrying since he had reached
the age of reason. He had been freed to follow God's will.
His feet felt firm on the earth because he now knew his
place and purpose. Doubt had vanished, replaced by faith.
Hope replaced despair and despondency. Self-hatred
turned to self-acceptance. Love replaced resentment toward the world and toward his father. Francis was made
anew, outside and inside, a make-over accomplished by
handing himself over totally to God.

And how did Pietro react? Unlike the father of the
prodigal son, there would be no homecoming, no adorning
his son in fine clothes again, no putting rings on his fingers,
no sandals for his feet, no party to celebrate the return of
a son who was thought dead but was now alive again. No,
Pietro understood that his dreams would never come true.
He had lost his son forever. And none of the legends and
biographies of St. Francis again mention Francis's father or
mother. They must have remained in Assisi, and perhaps
they saw their son from a distance, but there never seems
to have been any communication. Francis had chosen to
dedicate his life to his Lord, to the poor, and to rebuilding

San Damiano (and other churches). A simple life in imitation of Christ.

To understand what had happened to his son, Pietro, in William Blake's words, would need to "cleanse the doors of perception." To understand his son, he would need spiritual eyes, but his sight was fixed upon the image of a son that he and Pica had created: a son in *their* image. He truly could not see the son just reborn before him, the bishop, and all of Assisi.

This event in the piazza, however extraordinary it was, marked only a beginning. Francis would face many more hurdles, but at that moment he was ready to take a road less traveled, and it would indeed make all the difference—for himself and for untold millions who would follow.

3

Bellini's *St. Francis In The Desert*

Focus upon St. Francis's tunic. Its color represents the
earth. His feet are bare. He bears no emblems save the
bloody marks in his palms, the stigmata. When he shed his
father's clothes, he shed his former life. When he donned
the brown peasant tunic, he dressed himself in humility. In
the painting, his tunic is transformed, bathed in light, re-
flecting a way of life that leads to Christ. Francis has been
so completely remade in the image of Christ that he bears
the wounds of Christ's crucifixion and death.

Bonaventure describes the significance of the stigmata
that Francis bore:

> He marveled exceedingly at the sight of so
> unfathomable a vision, knowing that the
> weakness of Christ's passion was in no way
> compatible with the immortality of the se-
> raphic spirit. Eventually he understood from
> this, through the Lord revealing it, that Di-
> vine Providence had shown him a vision of
> this sort so that the friend of Christ might
> learn in advance that he was to be totally
> transformed into the likeness of Christ cru-
> cified, not by martyrdom of his flesh, but by
> the enkindling of his soul. As the vision was
> disappearing, it left in his heart a marvelous
> fire and imprinted in his flesh a likeness of
> signs no less marvelous.[14]

The cave behind Francis recalls the place where he
lived for a month, hiding from his father. The cave now
is not an escape but a path to more abundant life in God.
In the cave's darkness, Francis prayed to find the Light of
the World. In Bellini's painting, he has found the Light, a
heavenly brilliance that suffuses the whole painting.

Other painters convey the spiritual significance of light in different ways. In contrast to the heavenly light that fills Bellini's painting, Rembrandt's *The Return of the Prodigal Son* uses shadow, its colors muted in shadowy chiaroscuro.

Bellini does not use chiaroscuro because he is painting not an ordinary human being but a saint. To convey holiness he employs light that makes vivid every blade of grass, every leaf, every tree, every rock, every animal. They shine in the very light that fully enfolds and emblazes Francis's body. It is as if the sun is shining upon Francis and so upon everything around him; thus, the painting becomes a kind of icon, or what Roman Catholics call a "holy card." Bellini's painting is not a mere card used to mark one's place in a missal or prayer book, but a holy picture that imprints the image of the stigmatized St. Francis in our mind's eye. Francis becomes a permanent reminder of what is important in Christian life: Jesus Christ, the Light of the World.

4

Study Guide

Recite the St. Francis prayer.

Prayer of St. Francis

Lord, make me an instrument of your peace.
Where there is hatred, let me sow love.
Where there is injury, pardon.
Where there is doubt, faith.
Where there is despair, hope.
Where there is darkness, light.
Where there is sadness, joy.
O Divine Master, grant that I may not so much seek
to be consoled, as to console;
to be understood, as to understand;
to be loved, as to love.
For it is in giving that we receive.
It is in pardoning that we are pardoned,
and it is in dying that we are born to Eternal Life.

1. In reference to "The Canticle of the Creatures": When you think about the moon, what comes to mind?

2. In Francis's time, the moon signified mystery. How has modern lunar exploration affected your perception of the moon's archetypal significance?

3. Compare the modern understanding of and attitude toward the stars with that of Francis.

4. Describe the sense of creation that Francis captures in the Canticle. How do modern audiences see creation?

5. What does the Canticle offer a modern reader?

6. What mystical elements do you discern in the Canticle?

7. What other poets resemble Francis?

8. What explanation can you offer concerning Francis hearing Christ speaking from the cross in San Damiano?

9. How would you explain his subsequent actions?

10. What motivated Francis to take his father's goods and sell them?

11. Why did the curate of San Damiano refuse the money Francis offered?

12. What were Pietro's motivations in taking his son to court?

13. What role did Francis's mother, Pica, play in his life?

14. Why did Francis strip himself naked in the piazza?

15. How can Francis's actions in the piazza be applied to contemporary life?

16. What motivated Bishop Guido to side with Francis and not with Pietro?

17. What is positive about the rupture between Francis and his father? What is negative? What do these consequences say about both son and father?

18. What levels of meaning are there in Bishop Guido covering Francis with his mantle?

19. How can Francis's actions before the crowd be seen as an imitation of Jesus Christ?

20. How does Francis's "stripping" suggest actions you might take in your own life?

Chapter Three

Severance from His Family and Embracing the Leper

Be praised, my Lord, through Brothers Wind and Air,
and clouds and storms, and all the weather,
through which You give Your creatures sustenance.
Be praised, my Lord, through Sister Water;
she is very useful, and humble, and precious, and pure.

"The Canticle of the Creatures"

1

The Canticle of the Creatures

Even though wind cannot be grasped or seen, by calling it "Brother" Francis suggests familial intimacy. He could feel the wind blow around or past his body, ruffling his clothes; observe it fluttering the leaves of a tree, bending blades of grass, pushing clouds across the sky, scattering fallen leaves across the ground. Like God himself, the wind is always present.

The wind has productive work to do. It scatters seeds, it moves rain, it cools the earth and its inhabitants. It affects all kinds of weather. It is faithful; it always remains. For Francis, the wind recalls the Holy Spirit.

Francis surely recognized allusions to wind in the Bible, such as: "The wicked are . . . like chaff that the wind drives away" (Ps 1:4); "The wind blows where it chooses, and you hear the sound of it, but you do not know where it comes from or where it goes" (Jn 3:8). And, of course, Francis would have connected Brother Wind with the first wind, the breath God breathed into Adam, bringing him to life.

Francis calls water "Sister." Most cultural myths portray water as feminine because it possesses qualities and capabilities often associated with women: It is gentle. It cleanses. It nurtures. It quenches thirst. It is medicinal. It helps seeds and plants grow. Women bring forth new life; so do the living waters.

Having lived as a beggar for almost twenty years before he composed "The Canticle of the Creatures" (it is also a hymn, for Francis also composed music to accompany his verse), Francis was ever thankful for each cup of clean water, especially during the scorching Umbrian summers. With water he cleansed the sores of the many lepers he nursed in his lifetime. And water helped sustain his friars, for every Franciscan locus maintained a small farm.

Water brought to his mind Christ's baptism in the Jordan. Water also reminded him of those who cleansed Christ's tortured body, flayed with whips, pierced by nails, thorns, and lance. He surely remembered Christ's poignant words, "I thirst." He also must have been thinking of St. Clare's sisters, devoted to caring for the sick and dying at the San Damiano hospital, the center of their Order. So Francis certainly drew on many images and experiences in calling water "Sister." Christ's words sum up all these images: "Very truly, I tell you, no one can enter the kingdom of God without being born of water and Spirit" (Jn 3:5).

And Francis also knew the many other references to water in John's Gospel:

But those who drink of the water that I will give them will never be thirsty. The water that I will give will become in them a spring of water gushing up to eternal life. **(4:14)**

Let anyone who is thirsty come to me, and let the one who believes in me drink. As the scripture has said, "Out of the believer's heart shall flow rivers of living water." (7:37-38)

2

Biography

After the event in the piazza, Bishop Guido gave Francis a hermit's threadbare tunic. Wearing it, he set off on his new life. "New" clothes meant a new man. He put on what lepers generally wore: *tintinallo*, a cheap, rough, grayish-colored cloth containing very little wool. His clothing signified his putting on Christ's command to follow, and so leave everything behind. A person who decides to follow Christ first has to say farewell to his family: "they will be divided: father against son and son against father. . ." (Lk 12:53). To the young man who asked to bid his family farewell, Christ said, "No one who puts a hand to the plough and looks back is fit for the kingdom of God" (Lk 9:62).

Christ's words might seem insensitive or even harsh. But he understands human nature, how easily people can fall back into familiar habits. Starting a new life means not looking back. The past is *terra cognita*, the known, the future *terra incognita*, territory unknown. People are comfortable with what they know. Thus, when Francis undertakes a new life, one offered to Christ and the poor, he turns his back on his family. He does not hate them. He loves them more than ever.

Francis surely realized how he had humiliated his parents when in public he stripped off his clothes and returned them to his father. He understood that he must have looked ungrateful and that the people of Assisi considered him a fool, but he was willing to be God's fool. And today, to follow Christ demands courage just like Francis's. Many intellectuals, sophisticates, and trend-setters consider Christians to be fools, to be stupid dupes. But following Christ requires the willingness to be rejected as the early Christians had been, even, as is still true in parts of today's world, to be tortured or killed.

To embrace a life devoted to Christ, a Christian some-times needs to make a spiritual pilgrimage. And Francis did so. In the Middle Ages, Rome and Jerusalem were the two most common destinations. (After Francis's death Assisi would become the third.) Rome contained the graves of the two great apostles, Peter and Paul. In traveling there, Fran-cis embarked upon two journeys—a physical one to the great city south of Assisi, and an inner journey of the soul.

From his early youth, lepers had terrified Francis. During the Middle Ages leprosy was common. It was dis-figuring and incurable, its awful sores filled with pus that gave off a terrible stench. Most people could not abide see-ing or smelling lepers, who were banished outside the city walls. They had to live in the countryside, usually in caves or in lazars, hospices the Church provided for them.

When lepers arrived at the lazar, a priest would pray over them, announcing that they were dead to the world, and then over them would sprinkle earth gathered from a grave. When lepers went forth begging for alms, they were required to announce their presence with loud clappers, called *tentennella*. They had to approach people downwind and were forbidden to drink from streams and rivers used by healthy people.

This horrible disease would be suffering enough, but lepers also bore additional opprobrium. Most people be-lieved that the disease was God's punishment for serious sins. Even in the modern world some look down on the poor, thinking that they are responsible for their pover-ty. At the beginning of the AIDS epidemic, some felt that those who had contracted the disease deserved it because of their sinful lives.

Francis, a refined young man, came from a family where cleanliness was a way of life. He could not abide lepers, dressed in filthy rags, their flesh eaten away. Because of his disgust and his belief that the disease was contagious he kept his distance, giving alms by throwing money toward them.

On his journey to Rome, Francis came upon a colony of lepers. He no longer had money or food to offer. He recalled his insensitive rejection of lepers, how he had sped in horror from them. But now what could he do? He had become nothing to the world, just like them, but he could offer his very nothingness. He approached one, kissed his hand, and embraced him. An embrace! How can someone who had been so terrified make this gesture? Surely Francis recalled that Christ touched lepers and cured them. He could offer no cure, but he could offer love. He could offer solidarity, for he too was now part of a group of "nothings"—of "no ones."

This embrace was a watershed moment in his life. In his *Testament*, he wrote,

> The Lord gave me, Brother Francis, thus to begin doing penance in this way: for when I was in sin, it seemed too bitter for me to see lepers. And the Lord Himself led me among them and I showed mercy to them. And when I left them, what had seemed bitter to me was turned into sweetness of soul and body.[15]

From a Jungian perspective what does that embrace mean? Carl Jung says that we all carry within us an archetypal shadow, a representation of the dark aspects of our personality, all the bad deeds we wish we had never done. The shadow represents the person we have no wish to be.

Francis's terror of lepers may represent a flight from his own shadow, his sinful self. He always reminded his brothers that in his youth he was a great sinner. Perhaps, projecting this sinful self onto lepers, he was acknowledging that it was not lepers themselves that frightened him but his own repressed shadow, not yet raised up into the light of consciousness. Thus, in embracing the leper he exhibits love, compassion, and acceptance for a suffering fellow human being, but he is also exhibiting love, compassion, and acceptance of himself, a significant stage in the process of his individuation (becoming a whole individual). He is becoming his True Self.

The archetypal shadow is a common literary trope. In Shakespeare's *The Tempest*, Prospero must control Caliban, the monstrous offspring of a witch, because Caliban is capable of great evil. At the end of the play, however, when Prospero has forgiven all who have betrayed him, he turns to Caliban and says, "This thing of darkness I acknowledge mine." Prospero integrates Caliban, a symbol of his dark side, by recognizing it and declaring possession.

At the beginning of Oscar Wilde's *The Picture of Dorian Grey* Dorian was innocent, pure, and good, but embraces evil in return for eternal youth and wealth. The more he sinks into sin, the more his once wonderfully beautiful portrait becomes gruesomely distorted and ugly. But evil must somehow reveal itself; although hidden in the attic, the picture becomes horrific—an image much like that of a leper.

In Western consciousness sin is ugly. Plato believed that beautiful people had beautiful souls. Those who are not physically attractive may well possess an evil spirit. Although modern sensibility rejects such thinking, the underlying impulse still remains.

Not only did Francis embrace the leper, he became the lepers' champion. As he began his missionary work he fed them, washed their sores, and treated them with love. At San Damiano, St. Clare established a hospital to serve lepers, and Francis's followers assisted in caring for them.

It is difficult for contemporary people to understand how revolutionary Francis's actions were. Just as Christ resurrected Lazarus, Francis "resurrected" lepers from the "dead." Like Christ, Francis extended his clean, healthy laborer's hand in love. And some legends claim he cured lepers. He may or may not have performed physical cures, but he did accept them, nurse them, and above all love them.

A more recent example of the revolution Francis brought comes from the 1980s. AIDS victims terrified people; many did not want to be in the same room with them, would not enter a restaurant where someone with AIDS may have eaten. At religious services, worshipers would sit pews away from someone they suspected might have AIDS. What would Francis have done? He would have withheld judgment. He would have done everything he could to relieve their suffering, their humiliation. At the end of their lives he would have held their hands, not letting them die alone. Many families rejected their own children with AIDS. Many died alone—in hospitals or in empty rooms or in the streets. Life today is not so distant from the thirteenth century; Francis still has much to teach us.

Francis journeyed to Rome alone. Later he would return to seek papal approval for his First Rule, but now he was on a solitary spiritual journey. His conversion at San Damiano, when his life took a substantial turn, was a solitary choice. Such loneliness is part of life. To find himself Francis had to separate himself from friends, from family, from Assisi. Such a solitary experience is frightening because human identity is interconnected with friends, family, church, city, and nation. But ultimately each of us is alone—with the Alone, with God.

On this journey, Francis also entered the darkness of his own being where his biographer says that he, like Moses at the burning bush, pondered the "blazing fire" of the gospel. Although literate, he was not a great lover of books, and had little access to them. What he knew of the gospel he had memorized from listening intently at Mass. When he did not understand a passage, Francis would approach the priest for an exegesis.

After traveling to Rome, Francis returned to continue rebuilding San Damiano. Since embracing the leper, he expanded his outreach to the poor, including the many lepers roaming the hills of Umbria. And he continued to pray and fast.

Francis could have become a hermit. In the Middle Ages monasteries flourished and there were many hermits. Abbeys prospered and the monks became well fed and lax in their spirituality. In disgust, many left the monasteries for remote places to live alone, depending upon charity for their sustenance.

Although Francis was a "people person," he always sought to pray and to fast alone. True contemplation demands solitude and silence. Francis, however, was able to marry the contemplative and the active life. He rebuilt several churches, continued to assist the poor, the ill, and the lepers, and preached throughout Italy and beyond.

After his pilgrimage to Rome he had no followers, nor did he seek any. He had devoted his life to God and it was enough. But many of his peers, young people searching for purpose and meaning, were watching him. They observed his voluntary poverty, his tenderness toward the poor and disenfranchised, and his gentle service to lepers. Many began to consider joining him.

Francis first thought of having followers after attending Mass one day. Thomas of Celano writes:

> One day the gospel was being read about how the Lord had sent out his disciples to preach. The holy man of God, who was there, in order to understand better the words of the gospel, humbly begged the priest after celebrating the solemnities of the Mass to explain the gospel to him. The priest explained it all to him thoroughly line by line. When he heard that Christ's disciples should not possess gold or silver or money, or carry on their journey a wallet or a sack, not bread nor a staff, nor to have shoes nor two tunics, but that they should preach the kingdom of God and penance, the holy man Francis immediately exulted

in the spirit of God. "This is what I want, this is what I seek, this is what I desire, with all my heart."[16]

On the day he heard this gospel, Francis stripped himself of his sandals, his staff, and his belt, and donned another tunic of rough material, the kind that chafes the skin like a hair shirt, as many holy monks often did. And he began in earnest to preach penance. Surely he must have been thinking of disciples, because preaching throughout Assisi and beyond was more than one person could do. He would need help, and it arrived.

The first to follow him was Bernard, from a prosperous Assisi family; he renounced his wealth to follow Francis. Then two more, Giles and Philip. Francis was moved by their willingness to pursue the difficult life he led, and with them he was able to finish rebuilding San Damiano more quickly and begin work on two other ruined churches. With these three, the Franciscan Movement was launched.

At this point, who has Francis become? He is on fire with love of God and with all his heart wants to follow in the footsteps of Jesus Christ. He had no inkling that spiritual movements proliferate to such a degree that the founder often loses control of what he has set in motion. At first, Francis did not want his group to be called a religious order and sought to avoid that happening. But he could not keep his mission as simple as the gospel message that had touched him so deeply.

The first Franciscans practiced pure Christianity. They went about their work without ecclesiastical approval. They answered only to God, certainly not to civil or religious authority. But to continue their mission, they would have to work within those power structures. Therein lies a mirror of Christianity in general. Christianity has never really been practiced as Christ presented it. As G.K. Chesterton noted, "The Christian ideal has not been tried and found wanting. It has been found difficult; and left untried."[17] To survive, the Church accommodates itself to the secular world. For instance, although Christ enjoined his followers to "turn the other cheek," the Church did not follow this dictum to the letter. As it became more involved in secular political life it also entered the affairs of the world, including armed combat. In order to apply Christian principles in complex social realities, theologians formulated the concept of "just war," although some members maintained a strict pacifism. The issue is too complex to tease out completely here, but it does illustrate how the Church and the great movements within it have always had to find ways of accommodating their original, pure concepts in order to incarnate Christianity in the world. Secular complexities intrude upon the pure inspirations that motivate founders, and this indeed happened to Francis and his original vision.

3

Bellini's *St. Francis In The Desert*

Francis devoted his life to caring for lepers, but Bellini's painting contains no hint of that. The body of St. Francis is presented as beautiful and radiant. The stigmatized hands suggest the crucifixion, but only gently. There is no sign of Christ's agony; his naked body striped with lashes; his head pierced with thorns, bloody rivulets flowing down his face. We see no reminders of people suffering from disfiguring disease, only a handsome figure rapt in wonder, his face not the least self-conscious because Francis is lost in God, absorbed in divine union.

Off to Francis's left lies a *memento mori*, a human skull. In the Middle Ages, it was common for monks to keep a skull in their cells to remind them of our common destination—death. Francis must have kept a skull for that purpose, but also as a reminder of the many lepers who died in his arms, lepers he touched and nursed.

Behind Francis is a cave, the locus of his prayer life, a place that provided the silence and the solitude necessary for contemplation. In its darkness he can be alone with his Lord. But the cave also suggests the places where lepers were forced to conceal themselves. They were considered the living dead, and so relegated to caves, openings into darkness that suggest graves.

Bellini's painting depicts Francis at La Verna by himself, but in fact he was accompanied there by three other monks, including Brother Leo, to whom he dictated many of his thoughts and inspirations, most notably his *Testament*. The painting depicts only Francis, but even if his brothers were there they would not be the ones to whom he felt close at this moment. He is a mystic and is in spiritual union with God through the stigmata, as well as through the natural beauty that surrounds him.

He is surrounded by God's creatures, both plant and animal, and above all by sunlight. "The Canticle of the Creatures" demonstrates how Francis never felt lonely. As the lilies of the field did for Jesus, the lowliest flower reminded Francis of God's omnipresence and beauty. The whole world was an open breviary, one Francis "read" whether he could see it or not. When he wrote the Canticle, he was almost completely blind; he knew the "breviary" of the natural world by heart. He fixed his eyes outward, whether fixed upon another person (in whom he saw Christ) or on God's omnipresent beauty. In the depths of his soul, he realized that God enters every moment of life. Like the sun, God fills with light every waking moment; like the moon and the stars, he enlightens the darkest reaches of our minds and souls.

The painting also includes animals. A rabbit is peeping out of a hole in the ground, its own cave. Christians adapted the rabbit, a pagan fertility symbol, to represent resurrection. Just as the spring fertility rite was transformed into the feast of Christ's resurrection and the renewal of life, so the white rabbit came to represent the virtues of gentleness, purity, and innocence.

In the background, to Francis's right, stands a heron. It represents the Passion of Christ because Christians believed that herons wept tears of blood. They were not birds of prey but peaceful creatures, echoing the greeting Francis always used, "May the peace of the Lord be with you."

Next to the heron is a donkey, which carried the frail Francis up to Mount La Verna. But it also brings to mind the beast of burden Christ rode into Jerusalem. Like Christ it is obedient, as was Francis, who heeded the voice that summoned him to rebuild San Damiano. In the distance is another Christ-image, a shepherd pasturing his sheep. Bellini's painting contains many emblems that represent two individuals who walked the earth—one simply a man, the other the God-man. Both are united in the mystical drama of the stigmata.

4

Study Guide

Recite the St. Francis prayer.

Prayer of St. Francis

Lord, make me an instrument of your peace.
Where there is hatred, let me sow love.
Where there is injury, pardon.
Where there is doubt, faith.
Where there is despair, hope.
Where there is darkness, light.
Where there is sadness, joy.
O Divine Master, grant that I may not so much seek
to be consoled, as to console;
to be understood, as to understand;
to be loved, as to love.
For it is in giving that we receive.
It is in pardoning that we are pardoned,
and it is in dying that we are born to Eternal Life.

1. Explain the mystical meaning of the sun in Francis's poem.
2. Why does Francis call wind "Brother" and water "Sister"?
3. How does Francis connect himself with wind and water? What does this connection reveal about him?

4.   Francis uses a literary device, *apostrophe*, to address natural phenomena like wind and water as if they were persons. What does apostrophe add to the poem?

5.   What do the wind and water have in common with the sun, moon, and stars, which Francis addressed in earlier stanzas? What does his relationship with the natural world reveal about Francis?

6.   Contrast the medieval attitude toward lepers with Christ's response to people with this disease.

7.   How is Francis's horror of leprosy more than a mere fear of contagion?

8.   In light of Christ's and Francis's actions on behalf of lepers, how can the disease be characterized as positive?

9.   What larger themes regarding St. Francis can be drawn from the Bellini painting?

10. What positive values can be inferred from the inclusion of a human skull in *St. Francis in the Desert?*

11. What is the significance of the animals in the painting? How do these details expand Bellini's theme regarding Francis?

Chapter Four

The Order and the Rule of St. Francis

Praised be my Lord for our Brother Fire,
through whom thou givest us light in the darkness;
and he is bright and pleasant and very mighty and
   strong.

"The Canticle of the Creatures"

1

The Canticle of the Creatures

He esteems all that provide light—sun, moon, and stars—
and so he praises fire. He calls fire "our Brother"; fire is
"very mighty and strong," traits generally considered masculine. Fire has positive, brotherly qualities—it provides
warmth against the winter cold. It enlightens hearths and
lamps, and in every Catholic church the constant flame before a tabernacle announces the presence of Christ. People
cook with fire and use it for medical purposes like steril-
ization or cauterizing. Francis once had to have a wound
cauterized, so he understood its power to inflict pain and
to heal. Still, Francis blessed the fire.

Up to age twenty-five, Francis lived mostly in spiritual
darkness. Only when Christ spoke to him from the cross
was he *enflamed* with a love of Christ. Just as cold suggests
a lack of passion, a lack of love, fire suggests the opposite.

Christ illuminates Francis's imagination: in his mind's eye Francis sees a rebuilt San Damiano, and because he is afire with inspiration, he works with passion and love to make that image a reality. Many looked upon him and his work with amazement or perplexity, for never before had they seen such spiritual passion in him.

His reference to "Brother Fire" also reflects scripture, with which Francis was familiar. In the Old Testament, Moses saw "an angel of the Lord . . . in a flame of fire out of a bush; he looked, and the bush was blazing, yet it was not consumed" (Ex 2:2). Jeremiah proclaimed, "Is not my word like fire, says the Lord, and like a hammer that breaks a rock in pieces?" (23:29). And Christ declared, "I came to bring fire to the earth, and how I wish it were already kindled!" (Lk 12:49).

Francis was afire with love for God and creation when he composed "The Canticle of the Creatures."

2

Biography

Like a blazing fire, Francis's radiant spirit and example drew many to him. They had observed him rebuilding churches, as well as feeding and caring for the poor. He did not preach erudite homilies, but the love of Christ overflowed from his heart. Astonished, they saw him care for lepers, washing and nursing them, eating from the same dish. He demonstrated such holiness that they acclaimed him a saint; the pope confirmed their observation just two years after his death.

The people of Assisi saw Francis dressed in a tattered tunic, walking barefoot, begging for food, working with his hands. They thought that Francis must have been forced out of his family. Otherwise, voluntarily to give up the wealth of his father, to sacrifice a career in the lucrative business of selling cloth, to renounce his noble friends—all these actions pointed toward lunacy.

However, some, like Bernard Quintavalle, sought to follow Francis and, like him, devote their lives to something higher than security and wealth. Bernard, one of the wealthiest men of Assisi, asked Francis if he could join him, but did not know how to divest himself of his possessions. Francis opened the gospel three times, and each time the passage mentioned giving up everything to follow Christ. Bernard took the message to heart and gave all his wealth away, becoming Francis's first follower. Peter Catanio, a friend of Bernard's and a trained canon lawyer, joined Francis as did Giles, an eighteen-year old farmer. All three remained with Francis the rest of their lives and gave rise to the Franciscan Order.

As he began his evangelical work, Francis had no intention of establishing an order. He had seen how power and wealth had corrupted other founders' purposes; he chose total dedication to God through vows of poverty, chastity, and obedience. Having seen how monks had become complacent and fat, he did not want to follow in their path. He wanted to live the purest kind of Christianity, following Christ's words exactly, and as his missionary work began and spread, he held true to that vision.

A year after rebuilding San Damiano, Francis had twelve followers. But because he had not gotten ecclesiastical permission to pursue his vision, he and his followers were charged with various kinds of heresy, primarily by clerics who envied Francis's charisma. Such charges could lead to excommunication, imprisonment, and even death.

Bishop Guido of Assisi, the very one who had covered the naked Francis with his own mantle, kept a protective eye on Francis and his group. Knowing that Francis needed protection, Guido advised him to go to Rome to seek Pope Innocent III's approval.

At first, Francis was reluctant. He wanted to follow Christ freely, not to subject himself and his little band to any bishop, cardinal, or abbot. He could preach anywhere and to anyone. But his way of life threatened not only the clergy but also many secular men of wealth and influence, like Francis's own father. Pietro, a proto-capitalist, sought to generate more and more wealth so as to live the good life. But his own son, Francis, would only accept men who renounced material goods. Guido understood how Francis's counter-cultural actions could appear threatening. To survive in a world where upward mobility was a sign of virtue, Francis would need the pope's approval.

In 1209, Francis and his men traveled to Rome, which had changed much from the city of emperors. At the height of its power, the city had a million people. Under the Caesars, Roman aqueducts supplied free, clean water to its inhabitants, free baths for cleansing and sports, clean and orderly streets, and an air of calm and order. By the thirteenth century, Rome had declined to 100,000 inhabitants with slums and hordes of beggars and thieves, many of them ill and homeless.

The fortunate ones who did remain—the pope, the cardinals, the bishops—possessed power and wealth. Bishop Guido, who was politically astute, explained to Francis that to continue his work, he would have to persuade the pope to permit it.

The first meeting went well. Francis impressed Innocent III with his sincerity and commitment to a single goal: to imitate the life of Christ. But Francis could not articulate his vision for the new order. Unlike the Benedictines, Cistercians, Augustinians, or other religious orders, he had not formulated a structure for his followers. Pope Innocent suggested that he take some time to think about his mission and to compose a rule.

Francis did not want to insert himself or his followers into the framework of a conventional religious order. His vision was to preach the gospel and help the poor and sick. In a second visit, in a stumbling fashion he was able to express his simple desire to follow Christ and to urge others to do so. Moved by Francis's simplicity and sincerity, Innocent gave Francis verbal approval to continue his work and preaching; he also informed Francis that he was to only inspire people to virtue and to follow the example of Jesus Christ, not to preach about doctrinal matters.

Francis quickly accepted the validation for which he had come to Rome. Now clerics could not criticize him; bishops could not banish him from their dioceses. He was happy; but like Bishop Guido, Innocent III was also politically astute—even brilliant. Before Francis and his men left the Lateran Palace, the pope ordered them to be tonsured, that is, to have their hair cut away from the middle of the head. Tonsuring was the first physical gesture in the process of being ordained a priest. By doing this the pope had officially designated them clerics, and therefore his servants—thus primarily not under Francis's authority, but the pope's. Although Francis must have understood this rationale and strategy, he did not envision—as Innocent III surely did—that in the next ten years his small band of friars would proliferate to over 3,000, and eventually become one of the Church's most numerous and powerful religious orders.

Innocent III, indeed, discerned the potential of Francis's dream and his vision. He understood that most Roman Catholics, especially the common people, were disenchanted with the Church and that Francis's vision would restore the faith because it could touch everyone, particularly the marginalized.

Francis did not have a sophisticated education; in fact, his distrust of intellectuals was the primary reason he declined Dominic's offer to merge his Dominican Order with Francis's. Dominic's mission was academic; Francis's was to the poor and uneducated. But Francis was intelligent, and he surely understood that one day he would lose control of his own movement, a loss that began on the day he and his followers were required to receive the tonsure. By the end of his life, Francis became more or less a figurehead, and the Franciscan Order came under the control of the very men Francis had always distrusted: ambitious intellectuals.

On his return to Assisi, Francis experienced one of the most famous events of his life: preaching to the birds. Thomas of Celano writes that upon seeing a great flock of doves, crows, and other birds, Francis approached. Since they did not fly away, he spoke:

> My brother birds, you should greatly praise your Creator, and love Him always. He gave you feathers to wear, wings to fly, and whatever you need. God made you noble among His creatures and gave you a home in the purity of the air, so that, though you neither sow nor reap, He nevertheless protects and governs you without your least care.[18]

Had he really preached to the birds? It is certainly a lovely, sentimental notion to imagine the gentle Francis preaching to them, an image still familiar among Franciscans and all who know them. But Francis ought not be sentimentalized. Although gentle and kind, he was tough-minded and understood human nature as well as the natural world. As Jim Littwin notes, "He was no mere romantic: he bled his prayers."[19]

It is likely that Francis did possess a mysterious empathy with animals of all kinds; somehow, in Wordsworthian fashion, he could "see into the nature of things," a rare gift granted to persons of great holiness. Bellini portrays a man caught in what Abraham Joshua Heschel calls "radical amazement." The expression on Francis's face suggests that he is beholding something amazingly wondrous and that all of nature is aware that something miraculous is happening. He stands in a luminous, dreamy landscape with his hermitage behind him. Even though gazing upon something unworldly, he is still of this world. To emphasize this, Bellini fills the landscape with physical images: animals, trees, bushes, vines, flowers, water, sky, with the sun shining upon all of it.

Bellini painted to fulfill two purposes—the devotional and the aesthetic. He wanted viewers to look deeply into his paintings, to let their eyes travel from one motif to another, each having symbolic purpose. And of course, he wanted them to appreciate beauty. Plato said, "You become what you behold." Beauty thus has a moral and spiritual purpose.

The painting includes all sort of animals, including sheep and the famous birds. Biographer Donald Spoto writes,

> Throughout the Middle Ages, birds were often used to represent souls, because they can fly up to God. They were also potent symbols of freedom. In the feudal system, the majority of people were tied to the land,

and almost no one was mobile. But birds
were unfettered, cheerful, singing, hope-
ful—everything workers aspired to be. . . .
The metaphorical point of the incident of
Francis and the birds, then, may well be that
in his preaching and in his fraternity, he often had more success with the lowest level
of society—the poor and disenfranchised
manual workers, poetically symbolized by
birds—than with the rich and powerful (the
clergy and nobility). This interpretation as-
signs Francis a far richer and more compas-
sionate sensibility than being simply a friend
of birds, and thus offers a view consistent
with his concern for and identification with
the poor.[20]

It would be improper to do away with the familiar stat-
ues of Francis with a bird in his hand or on his shoulder.
Surely he fed the birds and allowed them to come to him,
but Francis preached mainly to people—thousands of men,
women, and children, all poor, all in need of the hope that
Christ offers through gifted preachers and saints, Christian
exemplars like Francis of Assisi.

3

Bellini's *St. Francis In The Desert*

Why is Francis alone? His biographers note that to Mount La Verna he took his most trusted brothers, but Bellini portrays Francis as a lone figure to emphasize Francis's embrace of solitude. Embarking on a spiritual journey requires accepting one of life's hardest facts: we come into the world alone and we leave it alone. We also must accomplish our soul-making alone by entering the dark cave of our own being and traveling through "the labyrinthine ways of our own minds."[21]

After San Damiano Francis did not run away from facing himself. As the painting shows, he would leave everything behind and enter a cave's darkness, often not knowing what danger he might meet. Francis understood that our psyches too contain dangerous demons, but he had the courage to face the unknown. On many occasions he must have been terrified. Nevertheless, Francis remained kind and gentle. Although he toughened himself, he still felt fear.

He allayed that fear by placing his trust in God. The painting depicts him in a stance of surrender and acceptance, as if saying with his posture, "Lord, do with me what you will." Francis embodies Jesus Christ, as shown by the stigmata, which Francis indeed received, a miraculous event noted by all his biographers and confirmed by the Church.

Some scholars interpret Bellini's Francis as a figure of Moses who led his people out of Egypt. The donkey at Francis's right is an onager, a wild ass of the desert, and the bird below it, a heron, is native to the Nile River valley. The wooden structure behind Francis resembles a *sukkah*—a tent, hut, booth, or tabernacle—a portable structure that the Israelites used during their wanderings in the desert.

The hermitage behind Francis includes a wooden oratory desk, an opulent Bible resting on its face, and a skull perched atop. The desk's wooden crossbars suggest Christ's cross, the skull represents human mortality, and the Bible immortality. Behind the desk, a delicate cross with a crown of thorns transforms it into a meditation of Christ's sacrifice.

All the details of Francis's cave/hermitage are connected to wood: the willow fence, the wooden desk, and the vines. One of the vines bears grapes, suggesting the bread and wine that Christ turned into his Body and Blood. The symbolic grapevine also suggests the mystical union of Francis with Christ in receiving the stigmata.

Francis sought to lead his people back to Christ, back to the true and pure message of the New Testament. Like Moses he was a leader, and like Moses Francis would not live to see the Promised Land. He would die young, never knowing the extent and influence of his life or that of his order. In the portrait, however, Francis seems Christ-like because he appears transfigured. As Francis was transfigured, perhaps the lives of his own "apostles" were transfigured—for seeing Francis wounded and transfigured is also seeing Christ. Francis became Christ, and his brothers became Christ-like, like Francis.

Bellini's painting calls forth a similar dynamic in the minds and souls of its viewers. We certainly respond aesthetically, but also have a deeper experience, a plunge into the painting's spiritual implications. As we view this image, we too are "transfigured."

At the far left of the painting, below a slanting rock, a drainpipe emerges, water trickling from it. The flowing water suggests the underlying current that the painting depicts: Francis is being reborn. He died and was reborn in the waters of baptism, and on La Verna is born again as another Christ. The painting's imagery recapitulates what Jesus said: "Very truly, I tell you, no one can enter the kingdom of God without being born of water and Spirit" (Jn 3:5). Francis has followed in the steps of Christ, often barefoot, just as he stands on the earth of Mount La Verna.

4

Study Guide

Recite the St. Francis prayer.

Prayer of St. Francis

Lord, make me an instrument of your peace.
Where there is hatred, let me sow love.
Where there is injury, pardon.
Where there is doubt, faith.
Where there is despair, hope.
Where there is darkness, light.
Where there is sadness, joy.
O Divine Master, grant that I may not so much seek
to be consoled, as to console;
to be understood, as to understand;
to be loved, as to love.
For it is in giving that we receive.
It is in pardoning that we are pardoned,
and it is in dying that we are born to Eternal Life.

1. In the Bible, what does fire represent?
2. Why was Francis drawn to Brother Fire? What is
    the greatest value of fire in terms of our spiritual life?
3. What is the archetypal significance of fire?
4. How is fire associated with love?
5. How is love associated with enlightenment?

6. How is Francis's view of fire different from that of the pagans of Rome?

7. We live in an era when human beings have unleashed atomic power and have changed the world's climate. Has fire come to represent something different now than it did in the Middle Ages?

8. What impact did Bishop Guido have on Francis and his vision of true Christianity?

9. What is the value of a structure like a rule for a charismatic life like that of Francis and his followers?

10. Why did Francis resist having a rule?

11. Why did Francis allow the pope to subject him and his followers to the tonsure?

12. How does Donald Spoto's explanation of the significance of birds in the Middle Ages deepen your interpretation of Francis and his preaching?

13. How does a sentimental view of the relationship between Francis of Assisi and animals misinterpret the reality of his actions?

14. How can St. Francis be made more relevant to the lives of present-day people?

15. How does Francis prefigure contemporary environmentalism?

16. In what ways is Bellini's portrait of St. Francis an icon of modern ecology?

17. What parallels does Bellini make between Francis and biblical figures?

18. What Old Testament allusions does Bellini's portrait contain? What New Testament allusions does it contain? What larger meaning do these parallels convey?

19. How does Bellini use a mundane detail like a drainpipe to convey a universal message?

20. How does a detail like the *sukkah* expand and enrich the possibilities for interpretation of the painting?

Chapter Five

The Final Years, the Stigmata, and Francis's Retreat at Mount La Verna

Be praised, my Lord, through our sister Mother Earth,

who feeds us and rules us,

and produces various fruits with colored flowers and herbs.

"The Canticle of the Creatures"

1

The Canticle of the Creatures

The epithet *Mother Nature* has become commonplace. Calling the earth "Mother" makes eminent good sense: like a mother, the earth provides all that we need in order to live—air to breathe, water to drink, food to eat. Mother Earth indeed "feeds us" and "rules us," showering us with "various fruits with colored flowers and herbs." With her gifts, Mother Earth nurtures each human being from a helpless baby to an adult with bones, sinews, and organs that have grown strong. She too is God's creature; therefore, all comes from God.

Notice the declension: Francis began his Canticle by praising the sun, and his journey has descended from stars and the moon to the earth. Francis preferred to walk in his bare feet, relishing his body's connection to Mother Earth. He chose a tunic whose colors are those of the earth (gray and brown). Also notice that Francis is pragmatic in presenting what Mother Earth does for us, but among her gifts he includes Beauty, the beauty of flowers. Thus, not only does she offer fruit (food) but also aesthetic delights like flowers.

Francis valued one virtue more highly than any other—humility (for him, poverty is not so much a virtue as it is a state of being). Humility derives from the Latin *humus*, ground or earth. Thus, to be humble is to be grounded, to be rooted; "to have one's feet on the ground" means to have common sense and knowledge of who one is. The proud are above themselves, above the earth, and their own minds above God. A person's ego can become so inflated that like a balloon it floats into the air, and like a balloon, a punctured ego causes a painful fall. The Book of Proverbs says, "Pride goes before destruction, and a haughty spirit before a fall" (16:18). Consider the myth of Icarus: not heeding his father's counsel, Icarus flew too close to the sun, the wax of his wings melting and causing him to fall into the sea and drown.

Francis has a profound connection with the earth. He did not prefer to live in the city, but in rural areas. To get closer to God, Francis climbed the Umbrian hills in search of quiet and solitary caves where he could retreat for days or even weeks.

The cave symbolizes a womb: within the dark mysteriousness of the cave, Francis would pray and fast to come into divine communion. His goal, of course, was a rebirth of his Christian ideals and his spiritual life. He knew remaining too much in the world could make people forget Christ's message. Thus, early on he understood the value of the solitude and silence that allowed him to communicate with the Alone, the ALL ONE. And when he emerged from his retreat, the radiance emanating from him invariably amazed his followers. St. Bonaventure writes about Francis and prayer:

> Since he was made totally insensible to earthly desires through his love of Christ, aware that while in the body he was exiled from the Lord, the servant of Christ strove to keep his spirit present to God by praying without ceasing, and thus he would not be without the consolation of his Beloved. For whether walking or sitting inside or outside, working or resting, he was so focused on prayer that he seemed to have dedicated it not only whatever was in his heart and body, but also his effort and time. Many times he was suspended in such an excess of contemplation that he was carried away above himself and experiencing what is beyond human understanding, he was unaware of what went on about him.
>
> That he might receive the infusion of spiritual consolations more quietly, he went at night to pray in solitary places. . . .[22]

Christ himself was the example Francis emulated. Christ journeyed into the desert to pray. In his last act before being arrested he retreated alone to the Garden of Gethsemane, where he prayed to his Father. Like Christ, Francis always had several of his brothers nearby who cared for him, provided food and drink, and of course, kept him company. Francis surely must have meditated upon Christ's sadness at finding his apostles asleep at Gethsemane: "So you could not keep watch with me for one hour?" (Mt 26:40). He experienced something similar when many of his followers were "asleep" to his original rule, which in the end they rejected and rewrote.

Francis's mission was also to awaken people from sleep, to alert them to the presence of Jesus Christ in their lives. Christ himself is also his model for a conscious apprecia- tion of Mother Earth. Christ said, "Consider the lilies, how they grow: they neither toil nor spin; yet I tell you, even Solomon in all his glory was not clothed like one of these" (Lk 12:27). In his meditation, Francis surely remembered himself, a merchant's son, the best-dressed of the young men, the flower of Assisi. And now he is dressed in the coarsest cloth, of an unostentatious earthy hue and a tex- ture that irritates the skin. As the flowers live, so does Fran- cis: God provides everything he needs. He owns nothing: an ideal he wanted to include in his rule, but it was rejected, a rejection that must have made him suffer greatly.

Francis's appreciation of the glory of God's creatures reflects not only his radical poverty but also his radical amazement. Ilia Delio writes, "For Francis all of creation became a theophany, a manifestation of the goodness of God. But the Canticle also represents a life-time of conver- sion, as Francis strove to be a brother to all things and to praise God in the cloister of the universe despite his suffer- ings, feelings of abandonment and darkness."[23]

2

Biography

One of the most important events in Francis's life was his journey to Egypt to join the Fifth Crusade, promoted by Pope Honorius III. Francis devoted his life first and foremost to converting people to follow in the footsteps of Christ. In the thirteenth century, the Catholic Church considered the religion of Muslims, whose military nearly conquered the Holy Land, to be its greatest enemy. Francis had no interest in military matters; he hoped that Christendom would somehow regain the ground upon which Christ had walked.

He was truly not well enough for a journey to Egypt. Although his health was frail, however, his will was strong and he insisted on the six-week voyage. He brought with him Brother Illuminatus, among others. The trip was horrendous. They had little food and water. People were so hungry they stole from one another, an act often punished by immediate death. The overcrowded conditions also caused the swift spread of disease and of lice, brought aboard with the ship's hordes of rats.

Francis arrived in Egypt hoping to convert the Muslim leader. But he found that he first would have to reconvert the Crusaders, who were so wanton they even kept prostitutes in their tents. He was appalled at their licentious lives but was shocked even further at their ineptitude. Al-Kamil, the nephew of Saladin, was out-maneuvering them on every front.

The Christian leader, Cardinal Pelagius, knew little about warfare yet insisted on designing the campaign. On several occasions al-Kamil presented generous conditions to end the war, even offering to return Jerusalem and relics of the True Cross to Rome. But Pelagius, to the chagrin of Francis and the Crusaders, stubbornly rebuffed all offers of peace.

Francis, realizing that God had brought him to Egypt not only to convert Muslims but also to end the war, sought Pelagius's permission to act as an emissary to al-Kamil. At first, Pelagius dismissed the request as madness, but Francis was so forceful and insistent the cardinal finally granted him permission. Pelagius considered it a suicide mission and expected that he would soon receive the heads of Francis and his followers on a platter.

Francis and his companions walked toward the besieged city of Damietta, fortressed so well that the Crusaders were continuously beaten back. At first the Muslims took Francis to be a Sufi, a member of a holy Muslim sect. So they arrived safely in the city and were immediately led in to meet al-Kamil.

To attempt converting a Muslim to Christianity usually meant instant death. But Francis was so humble and sincere that al-Kamil, being a holy man himself, recognized holiness in his visitor. Francis instinctively knew that continuing to try to convert al-Kamil was pointless, and so turned his expedition into a pursuit of peace: he had come, he explained, to end the war, the suffering of both sides and the bloodletting—the message al-Kamil wanted to hear.

Thomas of Celano offers another narrative of Francis's encounter with al-Kamil:

> Before he reached the Sultan, he was captured by soldiers, insulted and beaten, but was not afraid. He did not flinch at threats of torture nor was he shaken by death threats. Although he was ill-treated by many with a hostile spirit and a harsh attitude, he was received very graciously by the Sultan. The Sultan honored him as much as he could, offering him many gifts, trying to turn his mind to worldly riches. But when he saw that he resolutely scorned all these things like dung, the Sultan was over-flowing with

> admiration and recognized him as a man un-
> like any other. He was moved by his words
> and listened to him very willingly.[24]

Pelagius again refused any offers of peace. Francis had failed: he failed to convert, failed to become a martyr for Christ, failed to stop the war. Only one good remained for him: he asked al-Kamil permission to visit Jerusalem so that he could set his feet upon the ground where Christ walked. The Sultan offered Francis supplies for the journey to Jerusalem, and other gifts as well. When Francis refused the gifts, al-Kamil was even more impressed. Two men, one of the Christian West and the other of the Muslim East, left each other with friendship and respect.

Few accounts document Francis's visit to Jerusalem, where it is likely he visited the usual holy sites, which today are maintained by the Franciscan Order.

The problem of an official rule for Francis and his followers remained, even after the pope accepted the short rule of 1209. A modern analogy might help explain the situation. Imagine a young man who has founded a new company. At first, it is small, but through hard work ethic it begins to grow. Growth creates the need for more employees, and it becomes so large, it must be apportioned into departments, each department having its own head. As profits continue it becomes a huge corporation, so large that it requires additional superiors.

Francis's movement attracted more and more men; by 1219 there were 5,000 friars. Such a large group needed a rule, superiors, direction, and supervision. Someone would have to "train" the newcomers. Francis opposed having a codified rule. His rule is simply the Gospel. Sometimes he would drop ashes upon his head and use ashes to draw a circle around himself. He said nothing, but his sermon was eloquent: his actions "said" to his followers, "Learn of me, I am mortal, from dust I came and to it I shall return. It's the only rule you need: imitate me and you imitate Christ."

On his return from Egypt, he walked into a battle-ground. The order had divided into two factions—a conservative one wanted only to follow Francis, and a more ambitious one wanted to imitate the Dominicans, the Benedictines, the Cistercians, and the Augustinians. They wanted to establish schools and churches, as well as novitiates, and to appoint priors and abbots. In short, they wanted a hierarchy in which a friar could ascend to positions of power, ultimately to the highest clerical categories—bishops and cardinals. For Francis, the whole process was anathema.

Francis's Second Rule contained twenty-four chapters. By the time Cardinal Ugolini, the champion of the Franciscan Order, and other Franciscans were done rewriting that rule, they had reduced it to two chapters. Francis's hundred Gospel quotations and invocations were diminished to eight. The Third Rule, as it is called, was short, concise, and easy to memorize. Realizing he had been overruled, Francis finally consented to it. His "company" was now controlled by the "stockholders."

In 1223, Pope Honorius III sanctioned and blessed the Third Rule. Even this rule, however, which contains nothing that Francis had actually written, at least possesses his spirit. Like the light that permeates his "Canticle of the Creatures," and the light that pervades Bellini's *St. Francis in the Desert*, the holy radiance of Francis's spirit illuminates the Franciscan Rule.

Francis was reluctant to write a rule because he had only one: the Love of Christ, of God's creatures, including every human being on earth. Do you need a rule to feed the hungry, to clothe the naked, to minister to the sick? Do you need a rule to show compassion to lepers? Francis answered, "No." It was simple to become a Franciscan: pour forth love as God empties himself for us, and empty ourselves for others, an emptying that paradoxically pours out until "my cup overflows" (Psalm 23:5).

In his later years, suffering from many ailments, Francis moved to San Damiano where St. Clare's nuns cared for him. But he was still capable of traveling and delivering sermons. He spoke to great crowds, journeying as far as Bologna. Again, Francis was not known for his erudition, but he was a spellbinding orator because the Holy Spirit spoke through him. Even great theologians were impressed by his simplicity, his holiness, his spiritual insights, and his summons to follow in the steps of Christ.

Recall the episode when Francis stripped off his fine clothes and returned them to his father. This was his sermon par excellence, a sermon he preached without saying a word, a sermon he practiced every day of his life. On that day he embraced Lady Poverty. Afterwards he never owned anything. He wanted only to follow Christ. Stripping himself of his clothes, he stripped himself of ego and embraced a life of selflessness. And to become a follower it was necessary to follow his example, renouncing everything and embracing poverty, and then setting out into the world to practice and to spread the gospel of Jesus Christ.

Christ commenced his public life with twelve apostles and his movement grew and grew into the Church, which the creed calls "catholic"—that is, "universal." One divine man generated the Church. And one man, Francis of Assisi, generated a new spiritual order and movement that also spread throughout the world.

It is no wonder that many of Francis's followers wanted to establish schools—they wanted to learn other languages in order to spread their founder's message. The friars who early on had traveled to convert people in Germany returned to Assisi defeated because they could not speak German. To spread their movement the Franciscan Order had to learn the languages of other nations. They did, and it was a great day when the first Franciscan arrived in Oxford, for he certainly had to speak English!

But Francis was a simple man. Although visionary in certain matters, he was blind in others. To his credit, he finally transferred leadership of the order he founded to another. He was realistic, knowing it would be better for him and the order if he stepped down; when he did so, he fell to his knees before the new General of the order, Peter of Cattaneo, a person who had always been a loyal supporter, a person who was with Francis from the beginning, a person whom Francis loved.

3

Bellini's *St. Francis In The Desert*

Because Bellini's painting shows Francis in mystical union with Christ, it is also known as *The Ecstasy of St. Francis*. It depicts him receiving the stigmata. But prior to that union, he reveals his maturity as a mystic in his "Canticle of the Creatures."

Francis had an exquisite appreciation of God's handiwork, which he says deserves constant praise. Francis's reason for being was to praise God as revealed through, in, and by the beauty of nature. Francis understood that everything in its unique particularity glorifies God. Like the troubadour poets of his time who praised the women they loved, Francis praised his beloved divinity that revealed itself everywhere. His radical amazement at God's wondrous creation inspired Francis in 1224 to write the first Italian vernacular poem of genius, a century before Boccaccio (1313-1375) or Dante (1265-1321).

For our last meditation of Bellini's painting, let us pay even closer attention to it. The great twentieth-century French mystic Simone Weil notes that prayer is an act of pure, unmixed attention. Attention is like prayer because it demands self-forgetting. To look closely at anything requires being beyond self-consciousness; in fact, the ego must temporarily disappear.

For four weeks we have been examining the painting, and now let us look at it more attentively. Behind the *memento mori* of the skull appears a tall wooden cross encircled by a crown of thorns. Also notice the Bible on Francis's lectern. Above the Bible, four vines hold aloft clusters of grapes. Each of these alludes to Christ's passion. Also the lambs in the background, outside the city, suggest the *Agnus Dei*, the Lamb of God, Christ who willingly gave up his life for each of us.

Note the city in the background. It depicts Francis's home, Assisi. Bellini juxtaposes an urban setting and a rural or—although a barren landscape is not depicted—desert one. The painting includes flowing water, trees and plants, and animals not usually associated with the desert (although some argue that as a whole the painting is an allusion to the Old Testament desert). Bellini is underscoring the fact that Francis lived his life both in cities and in the country. He always preferred secluded, rural places—especially caves—where, if he so desired, he could retreat undisturbed to pray.

But why should we pay such close attention to art? A legitimate question. Does art really have anything to do with God or with spirituality? For a response, we turn to a passage from Pope John Paul II's 1999 "Letter to Artists":

> Within the vast cultural panorama of each nation, artists have their unique place. Obedient to their inspiration in creating works both worthwhile and beautiful, they not only enrich the cultural heritage of each nation and of all humanity, but they also render an exceptional social service in favor of the common good.[25]

For Bellini, painting was silent poetry. The artist puts those who pay close attention to a masterpiece like *St. Francis in the Desert* in touch with beauty. And because the source of all beauty is God, such a painting allows us to commune with divinity. God uses beauty to lure us to him. We need only submit ourselves to the beauty of "The Canticle of the Creatures," the beauty of the life of St. Francis of Assisi, and the beauty of Bellini's *St. Francis in the Desert* to be spiritually enriched, an enrichment that will affect our lives positively.

Bellini had a spiritual purpose in painting *St. Francis in the Desert*. A man of faith, he admired Francis and loved nature as had the saint. He would echo the Jesuit poet

Gerard Manley Hopkins, who said "The world is charged with the grandeur of God."

Art critics Joseph Godia and Denise Allen write:

> Giovanni Bellini renders the place of miracles, La Verna, with striking clarity so that those who view it might likewise believe, remember, and be inspired to follow the saint's spiritual journey. He portrays nature as luminous, sanctified through its creation by God—a perfect landscape that reveals even the smallest flowers as it grandly unfolds to include the towering mountains and skies that extend beyond what the eye can see. As we stand before the picture, Francis appears close to us; and the landscape around him encompasses us. Embraced by the saint's world, we witness his solitary vision.[26]

Examine Francis's face closely. Bellini depicts him with his mouth open and his eyes staring in amazement. He gazes at a six-winged seraph bestowing the stigmata upon him. Upon Francis's face is written the ineffable, and we can only try to imagine what is happening to him. But by attempting to understand Francis's life and the stigmata through the painting, we open ourselves to amazement, and possibly to what John Paul II calls an "epiphany of the inner beauty of things."[27]

4

Study Guide

Recite the St. Francis prayer.

Prayer of St. Francis

Lord, make me an instrument of your peace.
Where there is hatred, let me sow love.
Where there is injury, pardon.
Where there is doubt, faith.
Where there is despair, hope.
Where there is darkness, light.
Where there is sadness, joy.
O Divine Master, grant that I may not so much seek
to be consoled, as to console;
to be understood, as to understand;
to be loved, as to love.
For it is in giving that we receive.
It is in pardoning that we are pardoned,
and it is in dying that we are born to Eternal Life.

1. Many call Francis the "first ecologist." How might this be true?
2. How does "The Canticle of the Creatures" reflect Franciscan spirituality?

3. In what ways is Franciscan spirituality paternal? How is it maternal?

4. Francis emphasizes humility in the spiritual life. How did his observations of Mother Earth lead him to that perspective? How does he reflect Christ's admonition, "Learn from me, I am gentle and humble in heart" (Mt:11:29 NJB)?

5. How do you understand the term "ecology of the soul"? How does it relate to the usual understanding of the term "ecology"?

6. Why did Francis journey to Egypt?

7. Why does Francis make such an impression on Sultan al-Kamil?

8. What does it mean to "convert"? Besides a process of encouraging others to commit to another religion, how else can it be understood?

9. How was Francis's venture in Egypt a failure? How was it a success?

10. Discuss the significance of the various objects in Bellini's painting.

11. Bellini depicts a Bible upon Francis's lectern. Knowing what you do about Francis's life and character, why is this not biographically correct?

12. How does Bellini's painting relate to the celebration of the Mass?

13. The Latin word *humus*, meaning "ground" or "earth," connects to Francis's poem. How does it relate to the painting?

14. Why does Bellini juxtapose a city with Francis's cave on Mount La Verna?

15. What is the symbolic significance of a cave?

16. When Francis received the stigmata, he was with other friars, in particular Friar Leo, to whom he dictated

"The Canticle of the Creatures." Bellini, however, does not represent the observers. Why would Bellini have decided not to include witnesses in his painting?

17.   What might Francis's mother and father have thought had they witnessed their son receiving the stigmata?

18.   The most famous stigmatic of the twentieth century is Padre Pio. In the twenty-first century how would a miracle like this be considered?

19.   Some consider *St. Francis in the Desert* to be one of the world's greatest paintings. What artistic qualities lead viewers to value it so highly?

20.   Francis was canonized two years after his death. How does canonization reflect the social and historical needs of the people?

21.   What qualities do you think are essential for a person to be named a saint?

22.   Does aspiring to be a saint mean not accepting ourselves as we are?

23.   Some would call Bellini's painting propaganda, others a kind of visual sermon, others an expression of faith, and others a tribute. How would you describe *St. Francis in the Desert*?

Coda

During our journey with Francis of Assisi, we have not spoken much about Assisi itself. It continues to be one of Italy's great tourist attractions. It has much to recommend it—beautiful, warm summer days and an almost palpable holiness. When we walk the streets of Assisi, we feel as if we are walking upon holy ground. After a day of gazing upon Assisi's sky, hills, and landscape and watching Assisi's glorious sunset, we realize that we gaze upon the same beauty that held St. Francis spellbound, the very sight that inspired "The Canticle of the Creatures."

Assisi's narrow, winding streets bring to mind the way of life that Francis lived there as a boy and teenager. The town folk, many related to one another, loved to interact—talking, gossiping, singing, playing, selling their wares and celebrating the 150 holy days they considered important in their Catholic liturgical calendar.

Francis walked or ran up and down these very streets and byways. He was the *dominus* of his group of friends, the leader, because he was charismatic. Yes, he was wealthy, and he had "leaky" hands, giving away his money to friends and to beggars. He was indeed generous with what he received from his father, who paid for the wine Francis and his friends drank (and being young, they likely drank too much). And being young, they sang (mostly love songs) loudly and into the night when most of the people of Assisi had gone to bed. But when the neighbors realized that it was the charming Francis who was leading the revels, he of the beautiful voice who so lovingly sang the songs of the troubadours, they smiled and shook their heads in benign acceptance as they leaned out their windows to watch and to listen, or peacefully returned to their beds.

Like most children of Assisi, Francis was brought up in a household that spoiled him. His mother Pica—her name derived from Picardy, France, the land of her birth—was a good, pious woman. Socially she was a cut above her husband, Pietro. She probably spoke to her son in French; she even named him Francis after her native country, where Pietro made most of his money. Not only was Francis's father a successful cloth merchant, but also a clever real estate entrepreneur, owning many parcels of land outside the walls of Assisi. Thus, the little boy Francis was raised like a young prince, his every wish fulfilled.

In thirteenth-century Assisi a boy entered adulthood at fifteen. Francis, as his father expected, worked in Pietro's shop. He learned the value of textiles, their texture, place of origin, and the hierarchy from cheap wool to expensive silk and French brocade. He learned the value of money. If he had wanted, he could have followed in his father's footsteps as a businessman. But Francis wanted more. He was a dreamer and at first, as with many a young man, he had hoped to achieve fame as a soldier. He tried but failed. He also dreamed of becoming a knight. He tried that but failed. When he was twenty-two, it would have been difficult to imagine Francis becoming anyone extraordinary. He had become a ruined young man who once had great prospects but lacked the gifts necessary to make anything of them.

Then San Damiano—or, rather, Christ—entered his life. And Francis became a second Christ, a man who tried to follow Jesus, a man who tried to convert the world not by oratory, not by learning, not by power or wealth, but by example. He emulated Christ, and like Christ, said to his friends, "Come, follow me." In the beginning he must have been astonished at the number of men (and women, like Clare) who wished to follow him. Thus began the Franciscan movement. At first, Francis would have been satisfied to convert a few people to Christ. To win one soul is a lifetime's achievement, but Francis converted many. Countless people have been transformed by the life of Francis of Assisi, who is indeed known and revered throughout the world.

In Assisi his spirit still lingers. It is tangible. During World War II, in the spirit of St. Francis, Assisi saved eighty percent of its Jewish population—thousands of people—whereas Europe lost eighty percent.

The important figures for saving of Jews in Assisi are the Bishop of Assisi, Placido Nicolini, Don Aldo Brunacci, a diocesan priest and canon of the Cathedral of San Rufino, Colonel Valentin Muller, the sympathetic German commandant of Assisi and Franciscan friar, Rufino. Not only are they considered the saviors of the Jews in Assisi, but of the city itself.

We have much for which to thank St. Francis. He shows us how to live. He shows us how to be true Christians. He shows us how to be Catholics. He shows us, in short, how to be human. And not only Christians can learn from Francis. Every person is a child of God. Francis rejected no one. Like Christ, he loved all God's creatures. It is no wonder, then, that the whole world has embraced Francis of Assisi.

Late in his life he suffered many ailments and so was moved to San Damiano where Clare's nuns could care for him. When Francis returned from Jerusalem, he was very ill with tuberculosis, malaria, stomach ulcers, emaciation from his meager diet, and a disease that caused his eyes to bleed, rendering him sensitive to any kind of light. In this state of health, on Mount La Verna, Francis received the stigmata (on Michaelmas, 1224). This too caused Francis great pain. His biographer noted that when bathing Francis a friar accidentally touched one of his wounds and Francis rebuked him to be more careful.

His followers could not bear to watch him in pain. They sought medical help and Francis allowed the doctors sent by the Vatican to nurse him according to new practices. One was brutally painful: red-hot tongs were applied to his temples and red-hot pokers were inserted in his ears in the attempt to treat his eye disease. It was agony, especially for someone already in a terribly weakened condition.

He accepted invitations from bishops to stay with them but felt guilty for abiding in places of wealth and comfort. He was also invited to remain in Siena, but at heart he really wanted to return to Assisi's Porziuncola, the Church of St. Mary that he and his followers had rebuilt and that had become the headquarters of the Franciscan Order.

Realizing that he was dying, Francis articulated his feelings about death in stanzas later added to "The Canticle of the Creatures." They read:

> Praised be my Lord for all those who pardon one another for his love's sake,
>
> and who endure weakness and tribulation;
>
> blessed are they who peaceably shall endure,
>
> for thou, O most Highest, shalt give them a crown.
>
> Praised be my Lord for our Sister, the death of the body,
>
> from which no man escapeth.
>
> Woe to him who dieth in mortal sin!
>
> Blessed are they who are found walking by thy most holy will,
>
> for the second death shall have no power to do them harm.
>
> Praise ye and bless the Lord, and give thanks unto him
>
> and serve him with great humility.

Notice his unchanging spirit: no matter what happens, he prefers forgiveness and love over punishment and rejection, peace over tribulation, and endurance over complaint. For such a person, God, the most High, "shalt give them a crown."

Embracing the "death of the body," he calls death "sister." Why describe as feminine the event most people fear most? For Francis "sister" is emblematic of fulfillment. Life begins with the feminine, with our mothers, and so fittingly he bestows the feminine upon death; life comes full circle.

As a holy man, Francis was always aware of sin, especially "mortal sin." He warns against dying in sin, but implicit in his warning is the belief that God, like the now blinded Francis, is blind to our sins. Sins, in fact, bring us to God. That is why, twenty years earlier, Francis entered the Church of San Damiano. To seek forgiveness, not only from God, but also from himself,

Forgiving oneself is the hardest act. Yet we must forgive and love ourselves. This is not narcissism. It is a love authentically from God. We must love ourselves because God commands us to. Christ himself enjoined us "to love our neighbors as we love ourselves." To love another, we must love ourselves, and if we truly love ourselves, we will let God forgive our many sins.

Notice the last word of "The Canticle of the Creatures": "humility." This is the virtue that Francis values most. It is the virtue of the ground, the earth, and the rock. It is the virtue that reminds us that we are dust and to dust we shall return. It is the virtue that only one person who ever lived has the right to claim, Jesus Christ, who said, "I am meek and humble of heart."

There could be no better word to conclude one of the greatest poems ever composed nor a greater word for someone dying to pronounce: "humility." What more can be said to our Lord than, "I am your humble servant." And embedded within this simple statement is the virtue that St. Paul claims is indeed the greatest: love. "And now faith, hope, and love abide, these three; and the greatest of these is love" (1 Cor 13:13).

Francis's first biographer, the Franciscan friar Thomas of Celano, has the last word:

> His brothers and sons had assembled with the whole multitude of people from the neighboring cities, rejoicing to take part in such solemn rites. They spent that entire night of the holy father's death in the praises of God. The sweet sound of jubilation and the brightness of the lights made it seem that angels were keeping vigil.

> When day was breaking, the multitude of the city of Assisi gathered with all the clergy. They lifted his sacred body from the place where he had died and carried it with great honor to the city, singing hymns and praises with trumpets blaring. They all took branches of olive and other trees and solemnly followed the funeral procession, bringing even more candles as they sang songs of praise in loud voices.

> With the sons carrying their father and the flock following the shepherd who was hastening to the Shepherd of them all, he arrived in the place where he first planted the religion and the Order of the consecrated virgins and Poor Ladies. They laid him out in the church of San Damiano, home to those daughters he gained for the Lord. The small window was opened, the one used by these servants of Christ at the appointed time to receive the sacrament of the Lord's body. The coffin was opened: in it lay hidden the treasure of super-celestial powers; in it he who had carried many was now carried by a few.[28]

After San Damiano, St. Francis's body was carried to the parish where he grew up, the Church of St. George, a saint the young Francis loved because he slew the dragon. Then he was buried. All the inhabitants of Assisi and its environs were present to bid farewell to their saint, for they had already, according to custom, declared him so.

In 1228, two years after Francis's death, Pope Gregory IX confirmed the acclaim of the citizens of Assisi and declared Francis of Assisi a saint of the Roman Catholic Church. In 1979 Pope John Paul II declared him the Saint of Ecology, because of Francis's great love for God's creatures.

And in 2013 a pope first took the name Francis.

Dear St. Francis, pray for us.

For Further Reading

Armstrong, Regis J., OFM, J. A. Wayne Hellmann, OFM, and William J. Short, OFM, eds., *Francis of Assisi: Early Documents: Volume 1: The Saint*. New York: New City Press, 1999.

—— *Francis of Assisi: Early Documents, Volume 2: The Founder*. New York: New City Press, 2000.

—— *Francis of Assisi: Early Documents, Volume 3: The Prophet*. New York: New City Press, 2001.

—— *Such Is the Power of Love, Francis of Assisi As Seen by Bonaventure*. New York: New City Press, 2007.

Bodo, Murray, O.F.M. *Poetry as Prayer: St. Francis of Assisi*. Boston: Pauline Books and Media, 2003.

Cousins, Ewert, ed. and trans. *Bonaventure: The Soul's Journey into God, The Tree of Life, The Life of St. Francis*. New York: Paulist Press, 1978.

Cunningham, Lawrence, ed. *Brother Francis, An Anthology of Writings by and about St. Francis of Assisi*. New York: Harper and Row, 1972.

Englebert, Omer. Eve Marie Cooper, trans., augmented by Ignatius Brady, O.F.M. *St. Francis of Assisi*. Cincinnati: St. Anthony Press, 1965.

Foley, Leonard, O.F.M., Jovian Weigel, O.F.M., and Patti Normile, S.R.O. *To Live as Francis Lived: A Guide for Secular Franciscans*. Cincinnati: St. Anthony Press, 2000.

Green, Julian. *God's Fool: The Life and Times of St. Francis*. New York: HarperOne, 1987.

Horan, Daniel, O.F.M. *The Franciscan Heart of Thomas Merton*. Notre Dame, Indiana: Ave Maria Press, 2014.

House, Adrian. *St. Francis of Assisi: A Revolutionary Life*. New Jersey: Paulist Press, 2003.

Kazantzakis, Nikos. *Saint Francis (A Novel)*. New York: Simon & Schuster, 1962.

McMichaels, Susan W. *Journey Out of the Garden: St. Francis of Assisi and the Process of Individuation*. New Jersey: Paulist Press, 1997.

Merton, Thomas. *The Seven Storey Mountain*. New York: Harcourt, Brace & Co. 1948.

Murray, Wendy. *A Mended and Broken Heart: The Life and Love of Francis of Assisi*. New York: Perseus Books Group, 2008.

Rutherglen, Susannah and Charlotte Hale. *In a New Light: Giovanni Bellini's St. Francis in the Desert*. New York: The Frick Collection, 2015.

Sabatier, Paul. Jon M. Sweeney, ed. *The Road to Assisi: The Essential Biography of St. Francis*. Brewster: Paraclete Press, 2003.

Spoto, Donald. *Reluctant Saint: The Life of St. Francis*. New York: Viking Compass, 2002.

Talbot, John Michael, with Steve Rabey. *The Lessons of St. Francis: How to Bring Simplicity and Spirituality into Your Daily Life*. New York: A Plume Book, 1997.

Notes

1. James Littwin, "Bellini's Francis," with permission, February 10, 2018.

2. Regis J. Armstrong, OFM, J. A. Wayne Hellmann, OFM, and William J. Short, OFM, eds., *Francis of Assisi: Early Documents*: Volume 1, The Saint (New York: New City Press, 1999), 113.

3. Ibid., 201-02.

4. Attributed to Nicholas of Cusa, part of the Perennial Philosophy.

5. Armstrong, *The Saint*, 183.

6. Erik H Erikson, *Young Man Luther* (New York: W.W. Norton, 1958), 14.

7. Murray Bodo, OFM, *Poetry as Prayer* (Boston: Pauline Books and Media, 2003),15.

8. Paul M. Allen & Joan deRis Allen, *Francis of Assisi's Canticle of the Creatures* (New York: Continuum, 1996), 16.

9. Ewert Cousins, *The Soul's Journey into God, The Tree of Life, The Life of St. Francis of Assisi* (New York: Paulist Press, 1978), 191.

10. Wayne Hellman, OFM, Regis Armstrong, OFM, and Bill Short, OFM, eds., *Such Is the Power of Love: Francis of Assisi As Seen by Bonaventure* (New York: New City Press, 2007), 150.

11. Thomas Merton, *The Seven Storey Mountain* (New York: Harcourt Brace & Co., 1948), 116.

12. Susannah Rutherglen and Charlotte Hale, *In a New Light, Giovanni Bellini's St. Francis in the Desert* (New York: The Frick Collection, 2015), 99.

13. Armstrong, The Saint, 193-94.

14. Ibid., 201-02.

15. Ibid., 234.

16. Donald Spoto, *The Reluctant Saint: The Life of Francis of Assisi* (New York: Viking Compass, 2002), 103.

17. G. K. Chesterton, *What's Wrong with the World*, Part 1, "The Unfinished Temple," Chapter V, http://www.gutenberg.org/files/1717/1717-h/1717-h.htm.

18. Regis J. Armstrong, OFM, J. A. Wayne Hellmann, OFM, William J. Short, OFM, eds., *Francis of Assisi: Early Documents, Volume 2: The Founder* (New York: New City Press, 1999), 699.

19. Poet James Littwin, in a letter to the author.

20. Spoto, 119.

21. Francis Thompson, *The Hound of Heaven*. https://www.ewtn.com/library/HUMANITY/HNDHVN.HTM

22. Armstrong, et. al., *The Saint*, 231.

23. Ilia Delio, O.S.F., A Franciscan View of Creation: *Learning to Live in a Sacramental World* (New York: Franciscan Institute, 2003), 18.

24. Armstrong, et. al, *The Saint*, 284.

25. John Paul II, "Letter of His Holiness Pope John Paul II to Artists" http://w2.vatican.va/content/john-paul-ii/en/letters/1999/documents/hf_jp-ii_let_23041999_artists.html, 4.

26. Rutherglen and Hale, 133.

27. John Paul II, 6.

28. Armstrong, et. al, *The Saint*, 284.

New City Press

New City Press is one of more than 20 publishing houses sponsored by the Focolare, a movement founded by Chiara Lubich to help bring about the realization of Jesus' prayer: "That all may be one" (John 17:21). In view of that goal, New City Press publishes books and resources that enrich the lives of people and help all to strive toward the unity of the entire human family. We are a member of the Association of Catholic Publishers.

www.newcitypress.com
202 Comforter Blvd.
Hyde Park, New York

Periodicals
Living City Magazine
www.livingcitymagazine.com

For discounts and promotions go to www.newcitypress.com and join our email list.